MW01156786

HANS H. ØRBERG

LINGVA LATINA

PER SE ILLVSTRATA

PARS I: FAMILIA ROMANA
PARS II: ROMA AETERNA

LATIN-ENGLISH
VOCABULARY
II

DOMVS LATINA

MMI

LINGVA LATINA
PER SE ILLVSTRATA
by Hans H. Ørberg
PARS I: FAMILIA ROMANA
PARS II: ROMA AETERNA
INDICES
COLLOQVIA PERSONARVM
GRAMMATICA LATINA
EXERCITIA LATINA
PLAVTVS: AMPHITRYO
PETRONIVS: CENA TRIMALCHIONIS

Domus Latina, Hans H. Ørberg
Skovvangen 7, DK-8500 Grenaa, Denmark
www.lingua-latina.dk

Focus Publishing, Ron Pullins
P.O.Box 369, Newburyport, MA 01950, USA
www.pullins.com

A

ā/ab/abs *prp +abl* — from, of, since, by
ab-aliēnāre — turn away, alienate
ab-dere -didisse -ditum — hide
ab-ditus -a -um — hidden, remote
ab-dūcere — take away, carry off
ab-errāre — wander away, stray
ab-esse ā-fuisse — be absent/away/distant, fall short, be wanting
ab-horrēre ab — be inconsistent with
ab-icere — throw away
ab-igere -ēgisse -āctum — drive away
ab-īre -eō -iisse — go away
ab-olēre — efface, obliterate
ab-olēscere -ēvisse — be effaced/forgotten
ab-ripere — drag away, carry off
ab-rogāre — repeal, cancel
ab-rumpere — break off
abs *v.* ā/ab/abs
abs-cēdere — go away, withdraw
absēns -entis *adi* — absent
ab-solvere — free, acquit
abs-terrēre — frighten away, deter
abs-tinēns -entis — self-restrained
abs-tinēre -uisse -tentum — keep off
abs-trahere — remove, separate
ab-sūmere — consume, waste, destroy
abundāns -antis — overflowing, abundant
abundantia -ae *f* — overflow, abundance
abundāre (+*abl*) — overflow, be rich (in)
abundē — amply, more than needed
ab-ūtī +*abl* — use up, take advantage of
ac *v.* atque/ac
ac-cēdere — approach, come near
ac-cendere -disse -ēnsum — light, inflame
acceptus -a -um +*dat* — well-liked, popular
ac-cersere -īvisse -ītum — send for, fetch
accessiō -ōnis *f* — addition, accessory
ac-cidere -disse — happen, occur, be heard
ac-cingere — gird, *pass* gird oneself
ac-cipere — receive, get, hear
ac-cīre — summon, send for
ac-clāmāre — shout, proclaim
ac-colere — live near
ac-commodāre — fit, adapt
ac-cubāre — recline at table
ac-cumbere -cubuisse — lie down at table
accūrātē — carefully
ac-currere -rrisse -rsum — come running
ac-cūsāre — accuse
ācer -cris -cre — keen, active, fierce
acerbus -a -um — sour, bitter
acervus -ī *m* — heap, pile
aciēs -ēī *f* — line of battle, battle, sight
ac-quiēscere — go to rest, die
ac-quīrere -sīvisse -sītum — acquire, procure
ācta -ōrum *n pl* — deeds, actions
āctiō -ōnis *f* — action, delivery
āctor -ōris *m* — pleader, advocate
acūtus -a -um — sharp
ad *prp +acc* — to, toward, by, at, till
ad-amāre — fall in love with

ad-dere -didisse -ditum — add
ad-dūcere — lead, bring (to)
ad-eō *adv* — to such a degree, so, too
ad-esse af-fuisse (+*dat*) — be present, stand by
ad-hortārī — encourage, urge on
ad-hortātor -ōris *m* — one who encourages
ad-hūc — so far, till now, still
ad-icere — add
ad-igere -ēgisse -āctum — drive, compel (to)
ad-imere -ēmisse -ēmptum — take away (from), steal
ad-ipīscī -eptum — obtain
ad-īre -eō -iisse -itum — go to, approach
aditus -ūs *m* — approach, access
ad-iungere — join to, add, attach
ad-iuvāre — help
ad-minister -trī *m* — assistant, helper
ad-ministra -ae *f* — assistant, helper
ad-ministrāre — conduct, administer
ad-mīrārī — admire, wonder at
admīrātiō -ōnis *f* — wonder, admiration
ad-miscēre — mix (in), add
ad-mittere — let in, admit
ad-modum *adv* — very much, quite
ad monēre — remind, advise, urge
ad-monitus -ūs *m* — advice, prompting
ad-movēre — move near, put to
admurmurātiō -ōnis *f* — murmur
ad-nectere -xuisse -xum — attach, connect
ad-nītī — exert oneself, strive
adnotātiuncula -ae *f* — short note
adolēscere -ēvisse — grow up
ad-optāre — adopt
adopt(āt)iō -ōnis *f* — adoption
ad-ōrāre — worship, adore
ad-orīrī — attack
ad-ōrnāre — equip
ad-stāre — stand by
ad-suēscere — get accustomed
adulēscēns -entis *m* — young man
adulēscentia -ae *f* — youth
adulter -erī *m* — adulterer
adulterīnus -a -um — forged, false
adulterium -ī *n* — adultery
adultus -a -um — full-grown, adult
aduncus -a -um — hooked, curved
ad-vehere — carry, convey (to)
advena -ae *m/f* — immigrant, foreigner
ad-venīre — arrive
adventāre — approach
adventicius -a -um — from without, foreign
adventus -ūs *m* — arrival
adversārī — oppose, resist
adversārius -ī *m* — opponent, adversary
adversus/-um *prp +acc* — toward, against
adversus -a -um — facing, opposed, front, contrary, unfavorable
ad-vertere — turn, direct (towards)
ad-vocāre — call, summon
aedēs -is *f* — temple, *pl* house
aedificāre — build
aedificium -ī *n* — building
aedīlicius -ī *m* — ex-aedile

3

aedīlis -is *m*	aedile (magistrate)
aedīlitās -ātis *f*	aedileship
aeger -gra -grum	sick, ill
aegrē	with pain, unwillingly
aegrōtāre	be ill
aegrōtus -a -um	sick
aēneus -a -um	of bronze/copper
aequābilis -e	equal
aequābilitās -ātis *f*	equality
aequālis -is *m/f*	person of the same age
aequāre	make equal, equal
aequē	equally
aequinoctium -ī *n*	equinox
aequor -is *n*	surface, sea
aequus -a -um	level, equal, fair, calm
āēr -eris *m*	air
aerārium -ī *n*	public treasury
aerātus -a -um	fitted with bronze
aereus -a -um	of bronze/copper
aes aeris *n*	copper, bronze, money
aesculētum -ī *n*	oak forest
aestās -ātis *f*	summer
aestimāre	value, estimate
aestīvus -a -um	of summer
aestuōsus -a -um	sweltering, seething
aetās -ātis *f*	age, lifetime, life
aeternus -a -um	eternal, everlasting
aethēr -eris *m*	heaven, upper air, ether
aevum -ī *n*	time space, lifetime, life
affectāre	strive after, aspire to
affectus -a -um	affected by illness, ill
affectus -ūs *m*	mood, feeling
af-ferre at-tulisse al-lātum	bring, report, announce, bring about, cause
af-ficere	affect, stir, visit with
af-fingere	add, fabricate
af-fīrmāre	assert, affirm, prove
af-flīgere -xisse -ctum	cast down, deject, afflict
af-fluere	flow near
Āfricus -ī *m*	south-west wind
age -ite +*imp*	come (on)! well, now
ager -grī *m*	field
agere ēgisse āctum	drive, do, perform, act, spend, live, *pass* go on
agere (cum)	discuss, plead
agitur (rēs/dē rē)	is at stake
āctum est (dē)	it is all up (with)
agger -eris *m*	rampart
ag-gredī -ior -gressum	attack, set about, try
agitāre	move, stir, plan
(vītam) agitāre	live
animō/sēcum agitāre	think about, consider
agitātiō -ōnis *f*	brandishing
agmen -inis *n*	army on the march, file
agna -a *f*	ewe lamb
agnōscere -ōvisse	recognize
agnus -ī *m*	lamb
agrārius -a -um	agrarian
agrestis -e	rustic, boorish, *m* peasant
agricola -ae *m*	farmer, peasant
ain'	you don't say? really?
āiō ais ait āiunt	say

āla -ae *f*	wing
alacer -cris -cre	lively, eager, keen
ālātus -a -um	winged
albus -a -um	white
alere -uisse altum	nurse, feed, nourish
āles -itis *f*	large bird
aliās *adv*	at another time
al-ibī *adv*	in another place, elsewhere
alinēnigena -ae *m*	foreigner, stranger
aliēnus -a -um	someone else's
aliō *adv*	elsewhere
ali-quamdiū	for some time
ali-quandō	once, at last
ali-quantum	a good deal
ali-quī -qua -quod	some
ali-quis -quid	someone, something
ali-quot *indēcl*	some, several
aliter	otherwise
ali-unde	from elsewhere, from others
alius -a -ud	another, other
aliī... aliī	some... others
alius aliā viā	each in his own way
al-licere -iō -lēxisse -lectum	attract
al-ligāre	tie, fasten (to)
al-loquī	speak to, address
altāria -ium *n pl*	altar
altē	deep, deeply
alter -era -erum	one, the other (of two), second
altitūdō -inis *f*	height, depth
altum -ī *n*	the open sea
altus -a -um	high, tall, deep
alveus -ī *m*	trough
amāns -antis *m*	lover
amāre	love
amārus -a -um	bitter
amātōrius -a -um	of love
ambō -ae -ō	both, the two
ambulāre	walk
ā-mēns -entis	out of one's mind, mad
amīca -ae *f*	girlfriend
amīcitia -ae *f*	friendship
amictus -ūs *m*	mantle, cloak
amīcus -ī *m*	friend
amīcus -a -um	friendly
ā-migrāre	go away, remove
ā-mittere	lose
amnis -is *m*	river
amoenitās -ātis *f*	pleasantness, beauty
amoenus -a -um	lovely, pleasant
amor -ōris *m*	love
amphitheātrum -ī *n*	amphitheater
amphora -ae *f*	amphora (jar)
am-plectī -xum	embrace, cling to
ampliāre	enlarge
amplificāre	enlarge
amplitūdō -inis *f*	size, extent, greatness
amplius *adv comp*	more
amplus -a -um	large, big
amputāre	cut off
an	or, ... (really)? if

4

anceps -cipitis	double, undecided
ancīle -is *n*	sacred shield
ancilla -ae *f*	female slave, servant
ānfrāctus -ūs *m*	orbit (of the sun)
anguis -is *m*	snake, serpent
angulus -ī *m*	angle, corner
angustiae -ārum *f pl*	narrowness, pass, defile
angustus -a -um	narrow
anima -ae *f*	breath, life, soul, ghost
anim-ad-vertere	notice
animal -ālis *n*	animal, living being
animāre	give life to
animus -ī *m*	mind, soul, courage
in animō est (mihi)	I have in mind, intend
annālēs -ium *m pl*	annals
anniversārius -a -um	annual
annus -ī *m*	year
annuus -a -um	for one year, annual
ante *prp +acc, adv*	in front of, before
anteā	before, formerly
ante-capere	anticipate
ante-cēdere	precede, surpass
ante-cellere	surpass, excel
ante-ferre	prefer
ante-hāc	formerly
ante-īre	precede, surpass
ante-pōnere	place before, prefer
ante-quam	before
ante-venīre	forestall, anticipate
antīquitās -ātis *f*	antiquity, ancient times
antīquus -a -um	old, ancient, former
antrum -ī *n*	cave, cavern
ānulus -ī *m*	ring
anus -ūs *f*	old woman
ānxius -a -um	worried, worrying
aper aprī *m*	wild boar
aperīre -uisse -rtum	open, disclose
apertus -a -um	open
apis -is *f*	bee
ap-parāre	prepare, arrange
apparātus -ūs *m*	preparation, equipment
ap-pārēre	appear
appellāre	call, address
ap-pellere	drive, bring (to)
ap-petere	try to reach, seek, desire
ap-plicāre	attach
ap-pōnere	place (on), serve
ap-portāre	bring
ap-prehendere	seize
ap-probāre	approve
ap-propinquāre (+*dat*)	approach, come near
aprīcus -a -um	sunny
Aprīlis -is (mēnsis)	April
aptē	neatly, aptly
aptus -a -um	suitable, convenient
apud *prp +acc*	beside, near, by
aqua -ae *f*	water
aquārī	fetch water
aquātor -ōris *m*	one who fetches water
aquila -ae *f*	eagle
Aquilō -ōnis *m*	north (north-east) wind
āra -ae *f*	altar
arānea -ae *f*	spider, cobweb
arāre	plow
arātor -ōris *m*	plowman
arātrum -ī *n*	plow
arbiter -trī *m*	eyewitness, arbitrator
arbitrārī	think, believe
arbitrātus -ūs *m*	choice, decision
arbitrium -ī *n*	decision, wish
arbor -oris *f*	tree
arcēre	keep away
arcessere -īvisse -ītum	send for, fetch
arcuātus -a -um	arched
arcus -ūs *m*	bow, (triumphal) arch
ārdēns -entis	burning, ardent
ārdēre -sisse -sum	burn
ārdor -ōris *m*	burning, fire, ardor
arduus -a -um	steep
ārea -ae *f*	open space, site
argenteus -a -um	silver-, of silver
argentum -ī *n*	silver
arguere -uisse -ūtum	reveal, affirm, accuse
argūmentum -ī *n*	proof, argument
āridus -a -um	dry, barren
ariēs etis *m*	ram, battering ram
arma -ōrum *n pl*	arms
armāre	arm, equip
armātūra -ae *f*	armament, armed troops
armātus -a -um	armed
armentum -ī *n*	(herd of) cattle
armilla -ae *f*	bracelet
ar-rīdēre	smile at
ar-ripere	grasp, take hold of
ar-rogāre	claim
ars artis *f*	art, skill
artifex -icis *m*	craftsman, master, artist
articifium -ī *n*	skill, art, cunning
artus -a -um	close, tight, deep
arvum -ī *n*	(plowed) field
arx arcis *f*	hill-top, citadel
as assis *m*	as (copper coin)
a-scendere -disse	climb, go up, mount
a-scīscere -īvisse -ītum	admit, adopt
asinīnus -a -um	ass's
asinus -ī *m*	ass, donkey
asper -era -erum	rough, harsh, grievous
a-spergere -sisse -sum	sprinkle, scatter (on)
asperitās -ātis *f*	roughness, ruggedness
a-spicere	look at, look
assēnsus -ūs *m*	approval, assent
as-sentīre/-rī +*dat*	agree with, assent
as-sequī	attain to, achieve
as-serere -uisse -rtum	claim
as-sīdere	sit down
assiduitās -ātis *f*	perseverance
assiduus -a -um	constantly present
as-signāre	assign, allocate
as-sūmere	take, lay claim to
as-surgere	rise
astrologus -ī *m*	astronomer
astrum -ī *n*	star, constellation
asȳlum -ī *n*	refuge, asylum
at	but, yet, at least

āter -tra -trum — black, dark
āthlēta -ae *m* — athlete, prizefighter
atque/ac — and, as, than
atquī — but, and yet
ātrium -ī *n* — main room, hall, house
atrōx -ōcis *adi* — dreadful, atrocious
attat! — ah!
attentus -a -um — attentive
at-tenuāre — make thin, reduce
at-terere — wear (down), weaken
at-tinēre ad — concern, relate to
at-tingere -tigisse -tāctum — touch, reach, arrive at, adjoin
attonitus -a -um — stunned, stupefied
auctor -ōris *m* — originator, founder, advocate, guarantor
auctor esse — advise, advocate, relate
auctōritās -ātis *f* — authorization, authority
audācia -ae *f* — boldness, audacity
audāx -ācis *adi* — bold, audacious
audēre ausum esse — dare, venture
audīre — hear, listen
dictō audiēns esse — obey
au-ferre abs-tulisse ablātum — carry off, take away
au-fugere — run away, escape
augēre -xisse -ctum — increase
augēscere — grow, increase
augur -is *m* — augur
augurium -ī *n* — augury, omen
augustus -a -um — venerable, majestic
Augustus -ī (mēnsis) — August
aula -ae *f* — palace
aura -ae *f* — breeze, wind
aurātus -a -um — gilded
aureus -a -um — gold-, *m* gold piece
aurīga -ae *m* — charioteer, driver
auris -is *f* — ear
aurōra -ae *f* — dawn
aurum -ī *n* — gold
auspicārī — take the auspices
auspicium -ī *n* — omen taken from birds
Auster -trī *m* — south wind
austrālis -e — southern
aut — or
aut... aut — either... or
autem — but, however
autumnus -ī *m* — autumn
auxilium -ī *n* — help, assistance
auxilia -ōrum *n pl* — auxiliary forces
avāritia -ae *f* — greed, avarice
avārus -a -um — greedy, avaricious
ā-vehere — carry off, *pass* go away
ā-vellere -lisse -vulsum — tear away
avēre — be eager, desire, long
āversus -a -um — having the back turned
ā-vertere — turn aside, divert, avert
avidus -a -um (+*gen*) — greedy, eager
avis -is *f* — bird
avītus -a -um — of his grandfather
ā-volāre — fly off, rush off
avunculus -ī *m* — (maternal) uncle

avus -ī *m* — grandfather

B

baculum -ī *n* — stick
bālāre — bleat
balneae -ārum *f pl* — public baths
balneum -ī *n* — bath, bathroom
barba -ae *f* — beard
barbarus -a -um — foreign, barbarian
basilica -ae *f* — basilica
bāsium -ī *n* — kiss
beātus -a -um — happy
bellāre — wage war, fight
bellātor -ōris *m* — warrior
bellicōsus -a -um — warlike
bellicus -a- um — of war, military
bellum -ī *n* — war
bellus -a -um — lovely, pretty
bēlua -ae *f* — beast, wild animal
bene — well
beneficium -ī *n* — benefit, favor
benignus -a -um — kind, benevolent
bēstia -ae *f* — beast, animal
bēstiola -ae *f* — small animal, insect
bibere -bisse — drink
bibliothēca -ae *f* — library
bīduum -ī *n* — two days
biennium -ī *n* — two years
bīnī -ae -a — two (each)
bis — twice
blandīrī — coax, urge
blandus -a -um — charming, ingratiating
boārius -a -um — cattle-
bonum -ī *n* — good, blessing
bonus -a -um — good
bōs bovis *m/f* — ox
bracchium -ī *n* — arm
brevī *adv* — soon
breviārium -ī *n* — summary
brevis -e — short
brūtus -a -um — brutish

C

cachinnus -ī *m* — laugh, guffaw
cadere cecidisse — fall
cadūcus -a -um — ready to fall, perishable
caecus -a -um — blind
caedere cecīdisse caesum — beat, fell, kill
caedēs -is *f* — killing, slaughter, blood
caelestis -e — celestial, *m pl* gods
caelitēs -um *m pl* — gods
caelum -ī *n* — sky, heaven
caerimōnia -ae *f* — rite, ceremony
calamitās -ātis *f* — misfortune, calamity
calamus -ī *m* — reed, pen
calcar -āris *m* — spur
calceus -ī *m* — shoe
calida -ae *f* — hot water
calidus -a -um — warm, hot
callidus -a -um — clever, cunning
callis -is *f* — track, path
calor -ōris *m* — warmth, heat

campus -ī *m* — plain
cancer -crī *m* — crab, Cancer
candēlābrum -ī *n* — candelabrum
candidus -a -um — white, bright
candor -ōris *m* — whiteness, brightness
canere cecinisse — sing, crow, play, sound, sing of, prophesy
canis -is *m/f* — dog
cantāre — sing, sing of
cantus -ūs *m* — singing, music
capere -iō cēpisse captum — take, catch, capture, get, hold
capillus -ī *m* — hair
capitulum -ī *n* — chapter
capra -ae *f* — goat
captīvus -ī *m* — prisoner-of-war
caput -itis *n* — head, chief, capital, person, life, death penalty
carcer -eris *m* — prison
cardō -inis *m* — door pivot, hinge
carēre + *abl* — be without, lack
carīna -ae *f* — keel, ship
cāritās -ātis *f* — high price, love, esteem
carmen -inis *n* — song, poem
carō carnis *f* — flesh, meat
carpentum -ī *n* — two-wheeled carriage
carpere -psisse -ptum — gather, pick, crop
cārus -a -um — dear
casa -ae *f* — cottage, hut
castellum -ī *n* — fort, stronghold
castīgāre — correct, reprove
castīgātor -ōris *m* — one who reproves
castitās -ātis *f* — chastity
castra -ōrum *n pl* — camp
castus -a -um — chaste
cāsus -ūs *m* — fall, chance, accident
catēna -ae *f* — chain
caterva -ae *f* — band, troop, crowd
cauda -ae *f* — tail
caudex -icis *m* — trunk, blockhead
causa -ae *f* — cause, reason, case
   gen (/meā) + causā — for the sake of
causālis -e — causal
cautus -a -um — cautious
cavea -ae *f* — cage, coop
cavēre cāvisse cautum — beware (of)
cavus -a -um — hollow
cēdere cessisse — go, withdraw
cēlāre — conceal (from)
celeber -bris -bre — crowded, well-known
celebrāre — celebrate, extol
celebrātus -a -um — celebrated
celebritās -ātis *f* — crowding, reputation
celer -eris -ere — swift, quick
celeritās -ātis *f* — speed, swiftness
cella -ae *f* — temple chamber, chapel
celsus -a -um — tall
cēna -ae *f* — dinner
cēnāre — dine, have dinner
cēnsēre -uisse -sum — think, decide, assess
cēnsor -ōris *m* — censor (magistrate)
cēnsūra -ae *f* — censorship

cēnsus -ūs *m* — assessment, registration
centēsimus -a -um — hundredth
centum — a hundred
centuria -ae *f* — century (unit of 100)
centuriātus -a -um — voting in centuries
centuriātus -ūs *m* — office of centurion
centuriō -ōnis *m* — centurion (officer)
cēra -ae *f* — wax
cerebrum -ī *n* — brain
cernere crēvisse crētum — discern, perceive
certāmen -inis *n* — contest, fight
certāre — contend, fight
certē — certainly, at any rate
certō *adv* — for certain
certus -a -um — certain, sure
   certiōrem facere — inform
   certum mihi est — my mind is made up
cervus -ī *m* — stag, deer
cessāre — leave off, cease
cēterī -ae -a — the other(s), the rest
cēterum *adv* — besides, however
cēterus -a -um — remaining
charta -ae *f* — paper
chronic... ōrum (librī) — annals
cibus -ī *m* — food
cicātrīx -īcis *f* — scar
ciēre cīvisse citum — set in motion, move
cingere -nxisse -nctum — surround
cingulus -ī *m* — belt
cinis -eris *m* — ashes
-cipere -iō-cēpisse -ceptum
circā *prp* +*acc*, *adv* — round, round about
circēnsēs -ium *m pl* — games in the circus
circēnsis -e — of the circus
circiter — about
circu-īre -eō -iisse -itum — go round, outflank
circuitus -ūs *m* — rotation, circumference
circum *prp* +*acc*, *adv* — round, round about
circum-agere — cause to turn round
circum-dare — surround, put round
circum-dūcere — lead round
circum-fundere — pour/spread round
circum-īre -eō -iisse -itum — go round/about, outflank
circum-sedēre — besiege
circum-silīre -uisse — hop about
circum-sistere -stitisse — surround
circum-stāre — stand round, surround
circum-vāllāre — beset, surround
circum-vehī — go round, travel round
circum-venīre — surround
circus -ī *m* — circle, orbit, circus
cis *prp* +*acc* — on this side of
citātus -a -um — speeded up, swift
citerior -ius *comp* — nearer
citimus -a -um *sup* — nearest
citō *adv; comp* citius — quickly
citrā *prp* +*acc* — on this side of
citrō: ultrō citrōque — to and fro, on both sides
cīvīlis -e — civic, civil
cīvis -is *m/f* — citizen, countryman
cīvitās -ātis *f* — state, city, citizenship
clādēs -is *f* — disaster, defeat

7

clam — secretly
clāmāre — shout
clāmitāre — shout loudly
clāmor -ōris m — shout, shouting
clandestīnus -a -um — secret, clandestine
clāritūdō -inis f — fame, renown
clārus -a -um — bright, clear, loud, famous
classiāriī -ōrum m pl — marines
classis -is f — fleet, class (of citizens)
claudere -sisse -sum — shut, close, enclose
claudus -a -um — lame
clāva -ae f — club, cudgel
clāvis -is f — key
clēmēns -entis adi — mild, lenient
clēmentia -ae f — clemency, mercy
clībanārius -ī m — cuirassier
clipeus -ī m — round shield
clīvus -ī m — slope, sloping street
cloāca -ae f — sewer
co-alēscere -aluisse — grow together, coalesce
cocus -ī m — cook
coep- coept- v. incipere
coepta -ōrum n pl — undertaking, enterprise
co-ercēre — keep in control, restrain
coetus -ūs m — gathering, society
cōgere co-ēgisse -āctum — compel, force, summon
cōgitāre — think
cōgitātiō -ōnis f — thought, reflection
cognātus -a -um — related
cognitiō -ōnis f — getting to know, study
cognōmen -inis n — surname
cognōmentum -ī n — surname
cognōscere -ōvisse -itum — get to know, recognize
co-horrēscere -ruisse — shudder
cohors -rtis f — cohort, bodyguard
cohortārī — exhort
cohortātiō -ōnis f — exhortation
co-īre -eō -iisse -itum — come together, gather
colere -uisse cultum — cultivate, foster, devote oneself to, worship
col-lābī — fall down, collapse
col-lacrimāre — burst into tears
col-laudāre — commend, praise
collēctiō -ōnis f — collecting, gathering
collēga -ae m — colleague
col-ligāre — tie up, bind
col-ligere -lēgisse -lēctum — gather, collect
collis -is m — hill
col-locāre — place
col-loquī — talk, converse
colloquium -ī n — conversation, parley
col-lūcēre — shine
collum -ī n — neck
colōnia -ae f — settlement, colony
colōnus -ī m — (tenant-)farmer, settler
color -ōris m — color
colossus -ī m — large statue, colossus
columba -ae f — pigeon, dove
columna -ae f — column
coma -ae f — hair
comes -itis m — companion
cōmicus -a -um — of comedy, comic

cōmis -e — kind
comitārī — accompany
comitātus -ūs m — escort, retinue
comitia -ōrum n pl — assembly of the people
commeātus -ūs m — supplies, provisions
com-memorāre — mention
com-mendāre — entrust, commit
commendātiō -ōnis f — recommendation, praise
commentārī — think about, practice
commentārius -ī m — notebook, record
com-migrāre — move, go and live
com-mittere — engage (in battle), entrust, expose (to)
commodum -ī n — advantage, interest
com-morārī — stay, linger
commōtus -a -um — excited, passionate
com-movēre — move, excite, cause
commūnicāre — share
commūniō -ōnis f — partnership, sharing
com-mūnīre — fortify
commūnis -e — common
com-mūtāre — change (completely)
commūtātiō -ōnis f — change
cōmoedia -ae f — comedy
com-parāre (1) — prepare, provide
com-parāre (2) — compare
comparātiō -ōnis f (1) — preparation, provision
comparātiō -ōnis f (2) — comparison
com-pārēre — appear
com-pellere — drive, force
com-perīre -risse -rtum — find out, learn, discover
com-plectī -plexum — hug, embrace, surround, include
com-plēre -ēvisse -ētum — fill, complete
complexus -ūs m — embrace
com-plōrāre — lament, bewail
complōrātiō -ōnis f — lamentation
com-plūrēs -a — several
com-pōnere — settle, arrange, compose
compos -otis +gen — in possession of
compositum: ex c.ō — by prearrangement
compositus -a -um — well-ordered, compound
com-prehendere — seize, include
com-primere -pressisse -pressum — compress, crush, suppress, rape
com-probāre — approve, confirm
com-putāre — calculate, reckon
cōnārī — attempt, try
con-cēdere — go (away), yield, give up, concede, allow
concentus -ūs m — harmony
con-certāre — fight
con-cidere -disse — fall (down), collapse
con-cīdere -disse -sum — kill, beat
con-ciēre -cīvisse -citum — stir up, excite
conciliāre — win over
concilium -ī n — assembly, league
con-cipere — receive, catch, conceive
con-citāre — stir up, incite
concitātus -a -um — fast, rapid
con-clāmāre — shout, cry out
concordia -a f — concord

8

concors -rdis *adi* — harmonious, concordant
concubīna -ae *f* — concubine
con-cumbere -cubuisse — sleep (with)
con-cupīscere -īvisse — desire, covet
con-currere -rrisse -rsum — hurry together, clash
concursus -ūs *m* — concourse, encounter
con-cutere -ō-ssisse -ssum — shake
con-demnāre — condemn
con-dere -didisse -ditum — put, hide, found, close
condiciō -ōnis *f* — condition
conditor -ōris *m* — founder
cō-nectere — join together
cōn-ferre con-tulisse — bring (together), carry,
  col-lātum — confer, compare, apply
  sē cōnferre — betake oneself, go
  arma/signa cōnferre — join battle, fight
cōnfertus -a -um — dense, compact
cōnfessiō -ōnis *f* — admission, confession
cōnfestim — at once, immediately
cōn-ficere — make, accomplish, exhaust, subdue, kill
cōn-fīdentia -ae *f* — self-confidence
cōn-fīdere (+*dat*) — trust, be sure
cōnfīnis -e — adjacent, neighboring
cōn-firmāre — assure, encourage
cōn-fitērī -fessum — confess
cōn-flagrāre — be burnt
cōnflīctāre — harass, distress
cōn-flīgere -xisse -ctum — clash, fight
cōn-fluentēs -ium *m pl* — confluence
cōn-fluere — flow together, meet
cōn-fugere — flee for refuge
cōn-fundere — mingle, upset, confuse
cōnfūsiō -ōnis *f* — disorder, confusion
con-gerere — bring together, collect
con-gredī -ior -gressum — meet, join battle, fight
con-gregāre — bring together, gather
con-icere — throw, put
coniectūra -ae *f* — inferring, conjecture
con-iugium -ī *n* — marriage
con-iūnctiō -ōnis *f* — union, conjunction
coniūnctus -a -um — connected, associated
con-iungere — join, connect
coniūnx -iugis *m/f* — consort, wife
con-iūrāre — swear together, conspire
coniūrātus -a -um — sworn, joined by an oath
con-iūrātī -ōrum *m pl* — the conspirators
con-iūrātiō -ōnis *f* — conspiracy, plot
con-quiēscere — rest
con-quīrere -sīvisse -sītum — search out, investigate
cōn-salūtāre — greet, hail
cōn-scendere -disse — mount, board
cōn-scīscere -īvisse -ītum — decree, inflict (on)
cōnscius -a -um (+*gen*) — privy (to), accomplice
cōn-scrībere — enrol, compose, write
cōnscrīptī: patrēs c. — senators
cōn-secrāre — consecrate, deify
cōn-senēscere -nuisse — grow old
cōnsēnsus -ūs *m* — concord, agreement
cōn-sentīre — agree (on)
cōn-sequī — follow, overtake, achieve
cōn-serere -uisse -rtum — join

manum cōnserere — join battle
cōn-servāre — preserve, maintain
cōnservātor -ōris *m* — savior, guardian
cōn-sīderāre — observe, reflect
cōnsīderātiō -ōnis *f* — observation, reflection
cōn-sīdere -sēdisse — sit down, settle
cōnsilium -ī *n* — advice, decision, council, intention, plan, sense
cōn-sistere -stitisse — stop, halt
cōn-sociāre — associate, share
cōn-sōlārī — comfort, console
cōnsonāns -antis *f* — consonant
cōnspectus -a -um — conspicuous, remarkable
cōnspectus -ūs *m* — sight, view, survey
cōn-spicere — catch sight of, see
cōnspicuus -a -um — conspicuous, spectacular
cōnspīrātiō -ōnis *f* — agreement, conspiracy
cōnstāns -antis *adi* — steady, firm
cōnstantia -ae *f* — steadyness, persistence
cōn-stāre -stitisse — stand firm, remain, cost
  cōnstāre ex — consist of
  cōnstat — it is a fact, is is known
cōn-stituere -uisse -ūtum — establish, erect, set up, fix, decide
cōnstitūtiō -ōnis *f* — organization
cōn-suētūdō -inis *f* — custom, habit
cōn-suēscere -ēvisse — get used/accustomed to
  cōn-suēvisse *perf* — be accustomed
cōnsul -is *m* (cōs.) — consul
cōnsulāris -e — consular, *m* ex-consul
cōnsulātus -ūs *m* — consulate
cōn-sulere -uisse -ltum — consult, take counsel
  cōnsulere +*dat* — look after, take care of
cōnsultāre — deliberate, debate
cōnsultō *adv* — deliberately
cōnsultor -ōris *m* — adviser, counselor
cōnsultum -ī *n* — resolution
cōn-sūmere — use up, spend, exhaust
cōn-surgere — stand up, rise
con-temnere -mpsisse -mptum — despise, scorn
con-templārī — look at, observe
contemptus -a -um — despicable
con-tendere -disse -tum — strain, exert (oneself), hasten, contend
contentiō -ōnis *f* — tension, exertion, contest, comparison
contentus -a -um — content
con-ticēscere -ticuisse — fall silent
continēns -entis *adi* — unbroken, adjacent
continēns -entis *f* (terra) — continent
continentia -ae *f* — restraint, self-control
con-tinēre -uisse -tentum — keep, retain, contain
con-tingere -tigisse -tāctum — touch, be close to, (+*dat*) be granted to, happen
continuāre — continue, prolong
continuō *adv* — immediately
continuus -a -um — continuous, successive
cōntiō -ōnis *f* — meeting, assembly
cōntiōnārī — address a meeting
contrā *prp* +*acc, adv* — against, facing, on the other side, in return

9

contrā-dīcere — speak against, oppose
con-trahere — contract, wrinkle
contrārius -a -um — opposite, contrary
con-tremēscere -muisse — tremble, quake
con-tuērī — look at, contemplate
contumēlia -ae f — insult, affront
contumēliōsus -a -um — insulting, outrageous
con-turbāre — mix up, confound
cōnūbium -ī n — marriage, intermarriage
con-valēscere -luisse — grow strong, recover
convallis -is f — valley
con-vehere — carry, gather
con-venīre — come together, meet, be agreed, be settled
convenīre (ad/+dat) — fit, be fitting
conventus -ūs m — meeting
conversiō -ōnis f — rotation, revolution
con-vertere — turn, change
con-vincere — find guilty, convict
convīva -ae m/f — guest
convīvium -ī n — dinner-party
con-vocāre — call together
co-optāre — choose (as colleague)
co-orīrī — break out, arise
cōpia -ae f — abundance, means, control, pl resources, troops
cōpulāre — join, connect
cōpulātīvus -a -um — copulative
coquere -xisse -ctum — cook
cor cordis n — heart
cordī esse +dat — be dear/pleasing
cōram prp +abl, adv — before, in person
cornicen -inis m — horn-blower, bugler
cornū -ūs n — horn, wing (of army)
corōna -ae f — wreath
corpus -oris n — body
cor-rigere -rēxisse -rēctum — correct
cor-ripere — seize, rebuke
sē corripere — start up, hurry off
cor-rumpere — spoil, corrupt, bribe
corvus -ī m — raven
cotīdiē — every day
crās — tomorrow
crassus -a -um — thick, fat
crātis -is f — hurdle (of wickerwork)
creāre — create, appoint
crēber -bra -brum — frequent, numerous
crēdere -didisse -ditum — believe, trust, entrust
cremāre — burn, cremate
crēscere -ēvisse — grow, increase
crīmen -inis n — charge, accusation
crīminārī — accuse
crīnis -is m — hair
cruciāre — torture, torment
cruciātus -ūs m — torture
crūdēlis -e — cruel
crūdēlitās -ātis f — cruelty
cruentus -a -um — blood-stained, bloody
cruor -ōris m — blood
crūs -ūris n — leg
crux -ucis f — cross
cubāre -uisse -itum — lie (in bed)

cubiculum -ī n — bedroom
cubīle -is n — bed, couch
culīna -ae f — kitchen
culmen -inis n — summit, top, peak, roof
culpa -ae f — blame, fault, guilt
culter -trī m — knife
cultūra -a f — cultivation
cultus -ūs m — cultivation, care, mode of life, worship
cum prp +abl — with
cum coniūnctiō — when, as
cum prīmum +perf — as soon as
cum... tum... — not only... but also
cūnābula -ōrum n pl — cradle
cūnae -ārum f pl — cradle
cūnctārī — hesitate
cūnctātor -ōris m — one who hesitates
cūnctus -a -um — whole, pl all
cuneus -ī m — wedge
cupere -iō -īvisse — desire
cupiditās -ātis f — desire
cupīdō -inis f — desire, passion
cupidus -a -um (+gen) — desirous (of), eager (for)
cūr — why
cūra -ae f — care, anxiety, concern
cūrae esse +dat — be of concern
cūrāre — care for, look after, take care, undertake
curāre +acc., ger. — undertake
cūria -ae f — curia (division of the people, Senate-house)
currere cucurrisse — run
currus -ūs m — chariot
cursus -ūs m — running, race, journey, course, orbit, career
curvus -a -um — curved, crooked, bent
cūstōdia -ae f — guard, custody, post
cūstōdīre — guard
cūstōs -ōdis m — guardian, guard

D

dactylus -ī m — dactyl (—∪∪)
damnāre — condemn, sentence
damnum -ī n — loss
dapēs -um f pl — feast, meal, food
dare dedisse datum — give
sē dare — give oneself up (to)
dē prp +abl — (down) from, of, about, for, after
dea -ae f, pl dat/abl -ābus — goddess
dē-bellāre — finish the war, subdue
dēbēre — owe, be obliged
dēbilis -e — weak
dēbilitāre — weaken
dē-cēdere — go away, depart, die
decem — ten
December -bris (mēnsis) — December
decem-virī -ōrum m pl — commission of ten
decēre — be fitting, become
dē-cernere — decide, settle, fight
deciēs — ten times
decimus -a -um — tenth

10

dē-cipere — deceive
dē-clām(it)āre — make practice speeches
dē-clārāre — show, declare, express
dēclīnāre — decline, inflect
decor -ōris *m* — beauty, grace
decorāre — adorn, glorify
decōrus -a -um — handsome
dēcrētum -ī *n* — resolution, decree
decuma -ae *f* — tithe
dē-currere -rrisse -rsum — run down
decus -oris *n* — honor, ornament
dē-cutere -iō -cussisse -cussum — knock off
dē-decus -oris *n* — disgrace, dishonor
dē-dere -didisse -ditum — give up, devote
dē-dicāre — dedicate
dēditio -ōnis *f* — surrender, capitulation
dē-dūcere — lead/bring down, launch
de-esse dē-fuisse (+*dat*) — be missing, fail
dē-fendere -disse -ēnsum — defend, maintain
dēfēnsāre — defend
dēfēnsor -ōris *m* — defender
dē-ferre — carry, bring, report, confer, denounce
dē-fervēscere — calm down
dēfessus -a -um — worn out, tired
dē-ficere — fail, sink, wane, defect
dē-fīgere — fix, thrust, paralyse
dē-fīnīre — delimit
dē-flēre — weep for
dē-fōrmis -e — ugly
dēfōrmitās -ātis *f* — ugliness
dē-fugere — escape, avoid
dē-fungī — finish, have done, die
de-hinc — next, then
dē-icere — throw/bring down
dein — afterward, then
deinceps — in succession, next
de-inde/dein — afterward, then
dē-iūrāre — swear
dē-lābī — slip down, descend
dēlectāre — delight, please
dēlectātiō -ōnis *m* — delight, pleasure
dēlēre -ēvisse -ētum — delete, efface, destroy
dē-līberāre — deliberate
dē-līberātiō -ōnis *f* — deliberation
dēliciae -ārum *f pl* — delight, pet
dēlictum -ī *n* — misdeed, offence
dē-ligāre — tie up, fasten
dē-ligere -lēgisse -lēctum — pick out, choose
dē-linquere — misbehave, do wrong
dēlīrāre — be mad
dē-litēscere -tuisse — hide oneself
delphīnus -ī *m* — dolphin
dēlūbrum -ī *n* — temple, shrine
dē-mandāre — entrust, hand over
dē-mēns -entis — out of one's mind, mad
dēmere -mpsisse -mptum — remove
dē-mergere — sink, plunge
dē-mittere — let fall, drop, lower
dē-mōnstrāre — point out, show
dēmum *adv* — at last, only

dēnārius -ī *m* — denarius (silver coin)
dēnī -ae -a — ten (each)
dēnique — finally, at last
dēns dentis *m* — tooth
dēnsus -a -um — thick, dense
dē-nūntiāre — announce, order
dē-nuō — anew, again
deorsum *adv* — down
dē-pellere — drive down/off, avert
dē-pōnere — put/lay down, deposit
dē-populārī — sack, plunder
dē-populātiō -ōnis *f* — plundering
dē-portāre — convey, bring back
dē-poscere — demand
dē-prāvāre — pervert
dē-precārī — beg, entreat
dē-precātiō -ōnis *f* — entreaty, plea
dē-prehendere/-prēndere — seize, come on, surprise
dē-primere -essisse -essum — press down, sink
dē-prōmere — take out
dēpulsiō -ōnis *f* — rebuttal
dē-relinquere — leave behind
dē-rīdēre — laugh at, make fun of
dē-scendere -disse — go down, descend
dē-scīscere -īvisse -ītum — defect
dē-scrībere — draw, describe
dē-serere -uisse -rtum — leave, desert
dēsertus -a -um — deserted
dēsīderāre — long for, miss
dēsīderium -ī *n* — desire, longing
dē-signāre — mark out
dēsignātus -a -um — appointed, designate
dē-silīre -uisse — jump down
dē-sinere -siisse -situm — finish, stop, end
dē-sipere -iō — be out of one's mind
dē-sistere -stitisse — leave off, cease
dē-spērāre — lose hope, despair (of)
dēspērātiō -ōnis *f* — despair
dē-spicere — look down (on), despise
dē-spondēre -disse -sum — betroth, engage
dēstināre — designate, destine
dē-struere — demolish
dē-tegere — disclose
dē-tergēre — wipe off
dēterior -ius *comp* — worse
dē-terrēre — deter
dēterrimus -a -um *sup* — worst
dē-trahere — pull off
dētrīmentum -ī *n* — harm, loss
de-ūrere — burn
deus -ī *m*, *pl* deī/dii/dī — god
dē-vehere — carry, convey
dē-venīre — come, arrive
dē-vincere — defeat completely
dē-vincīre — bind
dē-vocāre — call away, divert
dē-vorāre — swallow up, devour
dexter -t(e)ra -t(e)rum — right; *f* right hand, the right
dicāre — dedicate
dīcere -xisse dictum — say, call, speak
diciō -ōnis *f* — dominion, power
dictāre — dictate

11

dictātor -ōris *m*	dictator
dictātūra -ae *f*	dictatorship
dictitāre	keep saying
dictum -ī *n*	saying, words
dictō audiēns esse	obey
diēs -ēī *m* (*f*)	day, date
in diēs	daily
dif-ferre dis-tulisse dī-lātum	postpone, defer, differ
dif-ficilis -e, *sup* -illimus	difficult, hard
difficultās -ātis *f*	difficulty
difficulter *adv*	with difficulty
dif-fīdere +*dat*	distrust, despair of
dif-fluere	overflow
digitus -ī *m*	finger
dignitās -ātis *f*	worthiness, dignity, rank
dignus -a -um	worthy
dī-gredī -ior -gressum	go away, depart
dī-lābī	fall apart, perish
dī-lacerāre	tear to pieces
dī-lātāre	spread, expand
dīlēctus -a -um	beloved, dear
dīlēctus -ūs *m*	recruitment
dīligēns -entis *adi*	careful, diligent
dīligentia -ae *f*	carefulness
dīligere -ēxisse -ēctum	love, be fond of
dī-lūcēscere -lūxisse	dawn, become light
dī-micāre	fight
dīmicātiō -ōnis *f*	fight
dīmidium -ī *n*	half
dīmidius -a -um	half
dī-mittere	send away, dismiss
diphthongus -ī *f*	diphthong
dī-rigere -rēxisse -rēctum	arrange, direct
dir-imere -ēmisse -ēmptum	divide, interrupt
dī-ripere	plunder, loot, rob
dī-ruere	demolish
dīrus -a -um	dreadful
dis-cēdere	go away, depart
dis-ceptāre	debate, discuss
discere didicisse	learn
dis-cernere	distinguish
discessus -ūs *m*	departure
disciplīna -ae *f*	instruction, discipline
discipulus -ī *m*	pupil, disciple
discordia -ae *f*	disagreement, discord
di-scrībere	divide up, distribute
discrīmen -inis *n*	distinction, grave danger
discrīptiō -ōnis *f*	distribution
dis-cumbere -cubuisse	take one's place at table
dis-currere -rrisse -rsum	run in several directions
disertus -a -um	eloquent
dis-icere	scatter, break up
disiūnctīvus -a -um	separative, disjunctive
dis-iūnctus -a -um	distant
dis-iungere	separate
dis-pālārī	wander about
dis-pār -paris *adi*	unequal, different
dis-pellere	drive apart
di-spergere -sisse -sum	scatter, disperse
dis-plicēre +*dat*	displease, offend
dis-pōnere	arrange, station
dis-putāre	argue, discuss
disputātiō -ōnis *f*	argument, discussion
dissēnsiō -ōnis *f*	disagreement
dis-sentīre	disagree
dis-serere -uisse -rtum	discuss
dis-sidēre -sēdisse	disagree, differ
dis-similis -e	unlike, different
dis-simulāre	conceal
dis-sipāre	scatter, spread
dis-suādēre	advise not to
di-stāre	be distant
di-stinguere -stīnxisse -stīnctum	distinguish, mark, characterize
dis-trahere	pull apart, break up
dis-tribuere	divide, distribute, share
districtus -a -um	busy
dītāre	enrich
diū, *comp* diūtius, *sup* diū-tissimē	long
diurnus -a -um	of the day, daily
diūtinus -a -um	long, prolonged
diūturnitās -ātis *f*	long duration
diūturnus -a -um	long, prolonged
dīversus -a -um	opposite, different
dīves -itis/dīs dītis *adi*	rich, wealthy
dīvidere -īsisse -īsum	separate, divide, share
dīvīnitus *adv*	by divine will
dīvīnus -a -um	divine
dīvīsiō -ōnis *f*	division
dīvitiae -ārum *f pl*	riches
dīvortium -ī *n*	divorce
dī-vulgāre	make public, divulge
dīvum -ī *n*	the open sky
dīvus -a -um	divine, *m* god
docēre -uisse doctum	teach, instruct, produce
doctor -ōris *m*	teacher
doctrīna -ae *f*	teaching, instruction
doctus -a -um	learned, skilled
documentum -ī *n*	example, proof
dolēre	hurt, feel pain, grieve
dolor -ōris *m*	pain, grief
dolus -ī *m*	guile, deceit, cunning
domāre -uisse -itum	tame, subdue
domesticus -a -um	domestic, household-
domī *loc*	at home
domicilium -ī *n*	dwelling, residence
domina -ae *f*	mistress
dominārī	be master, rule
dominātiō -ōnis *f*	dominion, power
dominātus -ūs *m*	dominion, power
dominus -ī *m*	master
domum *adv*	home
domus -ūs *f*, *abl* -ō	house, home
dōnāre	give, present with
dōnec	as long as, until
dōnum -ī *n*	gift, present, reward
dormīre	sleep
dorsum -ī *n*	back, ridge
dubitāre	doubt, be in doubt
dubitāre +*īnf*	hesitate
dubius -a -um	undecided, doubtful
n: sine/procul dubiō	without doubt, certainly

du-centēsimus -a -um	two hundredth
du-centī -ae -a	two hundred
dūcere -xisse ductum	lead, guide, draw, trace, construct, consider
uxōrem dūcere	marry
ductor -ōris m	leader
ductus -ūs m	leadership, command
aquae ductus	aqueduct
dūdum adv	a little while ago
duellum -ī n	war
dulcis -e	sweet
dum	while, as long as, till, provided that, if only
dum-modo	provided that, if only
dumtaxat	only, just
duo -ae -o	two
duo-decim	twelve
duo-decimus -a -um	twelfth
duo-dē-trīgintā	twenty-eight
duo-dē-vīgintī	eighteen
duplex -icis adi	double
duplicāre	double
dūrāre	harden, hold out, last
dūrus -a -um	hard
duum-virī -ōrum m pl	board of two men
dux ducis m	leader, chief, general

E

ē v. ex/ē	
eā adv	that way, there
ēbrius -a -um	drunk
ecce	see, look, here is
ecquid	...? if, whether
ec-quis/quī	(if) any(one)?
edepol	by Pollux!
ē-dere -didisse -ditum	emit, bring forth, make known, publish, do
ē-dīcere	decree, fix
ē-disserere	set forth, expound
ēducāre	bring up
ē-dūcere	lead out, draw out
ef-ferre ex-tulisse ē-lātum	carry/bring out, lift, elate
sē efferre	exult
ef-ficere	make, effect, cause
effigiēs -ēī f	likeness, portrait
ef-fringere -ēgisse -āctum	break open
ef-fugere	escape, run away, avoid
ef-fulgēre	shine forth
ef-fundere	shed, overflow, loosen
effūsus -a -um	disorderly, headlong
egēns -entis	poor, needy
egēre +abl	need
ego mē mihi/mī (gen meī)	I, me, myself
ego-met	I (myself)
ē-gredī -ior -gressum	go out, go beyond
ēgregius -a -um	outstanding, excellent
ēgressus -ūs m	going out
eia	ah! hey!
ē-icere	throw out
sē ēicere	rush out
ē-lābī	slip out, escape
ē-labōrāre	work out, prepare

ēlēctus -a -um	selected, picked
ēlegāns -antis adi	refined, skilful
elephantus -ī m	elephant
ē-līdere -sisse -sum	omit, elide
ē-ligere -lēgisse -lēctum	choose, select
ēloquēns -entis adi	eloquent
ēloquentia -ae f	eloquence
ē-loquī	express, tell
ē-lūcēre	shine forth
ē-lūcubrāre	prepare by lamplight
ē-lūdere	deceive, mock
ēluviō -ōnis f	flood, inundation
emere ēmisse ēmptum	buy
ē-mergere	come out, emerge
ē-minēre	stick out, project
ē-mittere	send out, emit, utter
ēmptor -ōris m	buyer
ē-mūnīre	fortify
ēn	look, here is
ē-nervāre	weaken, enervate
enim	for
enim-vērō	truly, certainly
ē-nītī -nīsum	strive, exert oneself
ēnsis -is m	sword
ē-numerāre	count up, enumerate
eō adv	to that place, there
eō abl +comp	so much
eōdem adv	to the same place
epigramma -atis n	epigram
epistula -ae f	letter
epulae -ārum f	meal, feast
epulārī	dine, feast
eques -itis m	horseman, knight
equester -tris -tre	cavalry-, equestrian
equidem	indeed, for my part
equitāre	ride on horseback
equitātus -ūs m	cavalry
equus -ī m	horse
ergā prp +acc	toward
ergō	therefore, so
ē-rigere -rēxisse -rēctum	lift, erect, cheer
ē-ripere -iō -uisse -reptum	snatch away, deprive of
errāre	wander, stray
error -ōris m	wandering, error
ē-rubēscere -buisse	blush
ē-rudīre	instruct, educate
ērudītus -a -um	well-instructed, learned
ē-ruere -ruisse -rutum	unearth, clear up
ē-rumpere	break out
ēruptiō -ōnis f	sally, sortie
erus -ī m	master
ē-scendere -disse	ascend, go up
esse sum fuisse futūrum esse/fore	be
ēsse edō ēdisse ēsum	eat
et	and, also
et... et	both... and
et-enim	and indeed, for
etiam	also, even, yet
etiam atque etiam	again and again
etiam-nunc	still
et-sī	even if, although

13

euax!	bravo!
Eurus -ī *m*	south-east wind
ē-vādere -sisse -sum	get out, escape, pass, turn out
ē-vānēscere -nuisse	vanish, disappear
ē-vehere	carry out, *pass* ride out
ē-venīre	happen, fall by lot
ēventus -ūs *m*	outcome, result
ē-vertere	overturn, overthrow
ē-vincere	persuade, bring about
ē-vocāre	call out, summon
ē-volāre	fly out
ē-volvere	unroll
ex/ē *prp* +*abl*	out of, from, of, since, after, according to
ex-aequāre	make equal
ex-agitāre	stir, worry, harass
ex-animāre	kill, *pass* die
ex-ārdēscere -ārsisse	flare up
ex-audīre	hear
ex-cēdere	go away, depart
excellēns -entis *adi*	outstanding
ex-cellere	be outstanding, excel
excelsus -a -um	lofty, high
ex-cerpere -psisse -ptum	pick out
excessus -ūs *m*	departure, death
ex-cidere -disse	fall out, be dropped
ex-cīdere -disse -sum	destroy
excidium -ī *n*	destruction
ex-cipere	receive, catch
ex-cīre -cīvisse	call out, summon
ex-citāre	wake up, arouse
excitātus -a -um	loud, shrill
ex-clāmāre	cry out, exclaim
ex-clūdere -sisse -sum	shut out, cut off
ex-cōgitāre	think out, devise
ex-cruciāre	torture, torment
ex-currere -rrisse -rsum	run out, rush out
excursiō -ōnis *f*	sortie, sally
ex-cūsāre	excuse
exemplar -āris *n*	pattern, model
exemplum -ī *n*	example, model
ex-ercēre	exercise, practice, worry
exercitāre	train, exercise
exercitātiō -ōnis *f*	exercise, practice
exercitātus -a -um	practiced, proficient
exercitus -ūs *m*	army
ex-haurīre	drain, empty, exhaust, endure
ex-igere -ēgisse -āctum	drive out, exact, require, pass
exiguus -a -um	small, scanty
ex-imere -ēmisse -ēmptum	take away, remove
eximius -a -um	choice, outstanding
ex-īre -eō -iisse -itum	go out
ex-īstimāre	consider, think
exitus -ūs *m*	exit, way out, end
ex-onerāre	unburden
exōrdium -ī *n*	beginning
ex-orīrī	rise, arise
ex-ōrnāre	adorn, decorate
exōrsus -ūs *m*	beginning
ex-pavēscere -pāvisse	become frightened (at)
ex-pedīre	make ready, extricate, explain
expedītiō -ōnis *f*	foray, raid, expedition
expedītus -a -um	ready for action
ex-pellere	dive out, expel
ex-pergīscī -perrēctum	wake up
ex-perīrī -pertum	try, experience
ex-pers -rtis *adi* +*gen*	having no share in
ex-petere	request, demand, desire
ex-plānāre	explain
ex-plēre -ēvisse -ētum	fill, complete, satisfy
explētīvus -a -um	expletive
ex-plicāre -uisse -itum	extricate, unfold, explain
ex-plōrāre	reconnoitre, investigate
explōrātor -ōris *m*	scout, spy
ex-pōnere	put out, put ashore, expose
ex-portāre	export
ex-poscere	ask for, demand
ex-pugnāre	conquer
ex-pugnātiō -ōnis *f*	conquest
ex-quīrere -sivisse -situm	ask about, examine
exquīsītus -a -um	studied, meticulous
ex-sanguis -e	bloodless, lifeless
ex-scindere	demolish, destroy
exsecrandus -a -um	accursed
ex-secrārī	curse
ex-sequī	pursue, go on, execute
exsequiae -ae *f pl*	funeral
ex-silīre -uisse	jump up
exsilium -ī *n*	exile
ex-sistere -stitisse	appear, arise
ex-solvere	set free, release
ex-spectāre	wait (for), expect
exspectātiō -ōnis *f*	exspectation
ex-spīrāre	breathe one's last, die
ex-stimulāre	stir up, incite
ex-stinguere -stīnxisse -stīnctum	extinguish, put out, kill, annihilate
ex-struere	erect, build
exsul -is *m/f*	banished person, exile
ex-sulāre	live in exile
ex-sultāre	rejoice greatly, exult
ex-suscitāre	rouse, kindle
extemplō	at once
ex-tendere -disse -tum	stretch out, extend
exter -era -erum	external, foreign
externus -a -um	external, extraneous
ex-terrēre	scare, terrify
extimus -a -um *sup*	outermost, farthest
ex-tollere	raise, praise, extol
ex-torris -e	exiled, banished
extrā *prp* +*acc, adv*	outside
ex-trahere	pull out, extract
extrāneus -a -um	foreign, stranger
extrēmus -a -um *sup*	outermost, utmost, last, *n* end, utmost danger
ex-uere -uisse -ūtum	take off, deprive of
ex-ūrere	burn up
exustiō -ōnis *f*	conflagration
exuviae -ārum *f pl*	clothing, armor

14

F

faber -brī *m* — artisan, smith
fabricāre — forge, build, construct
fābula -ae *f* — story, fable, play
fābulārī — talk, chat
fābulōsus -a -um — fabulous, celebrated
facere -iō fēcisse factum — make, do, cause esteem, value
  facere +*gen* — esteem, value
facessere — go away, be off
faciēs -ēī *f* — appearance, form, face
facile *adv, sup* -illimē — easily, readily
facilis -e, *sup* -illimus — easy, complaisant
facilitās -ātis *f* — ease, complaisance
facinus -oris *n* — deed, act, misdeed
factiō -ōnis *f* — party, faction
factiōsus -a -um — factious, scheming
factum -ī *n* — deed, act
factus -a -um — wrought
facultās -ātis *f* — possibility, *pl* resources
fācundus -a -um — eloquent
fallāx -ācis *adi* — deceitful
fallere fefellisse falsum — deceive, fail to keep
falsus -a -um, *adv* -ō — false, deceived, wrong
falx -cis *f* — sickle
fāma -ae *f* — rumor, reputation
famēs -is *f* — hunger, famine
familia -ae *f* — household, family, slaves
familiāris -e — intimate, *m* close friend
famula -ae *f* — servant-girl, maid
famulus -ī *m* — servant, slave
fānum -ī *n* — shrine, consecrated spot
fārī — speak
fās *n indēcl* — divine law, right
  fās est — it is right, it is allowed
fascēs -ium *m pl* — bundle of rods, fasces
fāstī -ōrum *m pl* — list of festivals, calendar
fāstus -a -um: diēs fāstus — court-day, workday
fātālis -e — fateful, destined
fatērī fassum — admit, confess, profess
fatīgāre — tire out, weary, worry
fātum -ī *n* — fate, destiny, death
faucēs -ium *f pl* — pass, defile
faustus -a -um — fortunate, favorable
fautor -ōris *m* — supporter
favēre fāvisse +*dat* — favor, support
favor -ōris *m* — goodwill, favor
fax facis *f* — torch
Februārius -ī (mēnsis) — February
fēlīcitās -ātis *f* — good fortune, luck
fēlīx -īcis *adi* — fortunate, propitious
fēmina -ae *f* — woman
fenestra -ae *f* — window
fera -ae *f* — wild animal
ferē — about, almost, usually
fēriae -ae *f pl* — festival days, holidays
fēriātus -a -um — keeping holiday
ferīre — strike, hit, kill
fermē — about, almost
ferōcitās -ātis *f* — fierceness, ferocity
ferōx -ōcis *adi* — fierce, ferocious
ferrātus -a -um — tipped with iron
ferre tulisse lātum — carry, bring, bear, endure, report, propose
ferreus -a -um — of iron, iron-
ferrum -ī *n* — iron, steel, sword
fertilis -e — fertile
ferus -a -um — wild
fervēns -entis — hot, boiling, ardent
fervere/-ēre ferbuisse — boil, seethe, swarm
fessus -a -um — tired, weary
festīnāre — hasten, hurry
fēstus -a -um: diēs fēstus — holiday, festival
fētiālis -e — fetial
fētus -a -um — having young
-ficere -iō -fēcisse -fectum —
fictilis -e — earthen, earthenware-
fictus -a -um — untrue, made up
fidēlis -e — faithful, loyal
fīdere fisum esse +*dat* — trust, rely on
fidēs -eī *f* — trust, faith, loyalty, promise
fidēs -ium *f pl* — lyre
fidicen -inis *m* — lyre-player
fīdūcia -ae *f* — trust, confidence
fīdus -a -um — faithful, reliable
fierī factum esse — be made, be done, beome, happen, result
fīgere -xisse -xum — fix, fasten, pierce
figūra -ae *f* — form, appearance
fīlia -ae *f, pldat/abl* -ābus — daughter
fīliola -ae *f* — little daughter
fīliolus -ī *m* — little son
fīlius -ī *m* — son
fīlum -ī *n* — thread, fillet
fingere fīnxisse fictum — form, make up, invent
fīnīre — limit, finish, delimit
fīnis -is *m* — boundary, end, *pl* territory
fīnitimus -a -um — adjacent, neighboring
firmāmentum -ī *n* — support, strength
firmāre — reinforce, strengthen
firmitūdō -inis *f* — stability, firmness
firmus -a -um — strong, stable, firm
fiscus -ī *m* — public treasury
flāgitāre — demand insistently
flāgitiōsus -a -um — disgraceful
flāgitium -ī *n* — disgrace
flagrāre — burn
flāmen -inis *m* — flamen (priest)
flamma -ae *f* — flame
flāre — blow
flātus -ūs *m* — blowing, breeze
flēbilis -e — plaintive
flectere -xisse -xum — bend, turn
flēre -ēvisse — cry, weep (for)
flētus -ūs *m* — weeping
flōrēre — bloom, flourish
flōs -ōris *m* — flower
flūctus -ūs *m* — wave
fluere -ūxisse — flow
flūmen -inis *n* — river
fluvius -ī *m* — river
foculus -ī *m* — brazier
focus -ī *m* — hearth
foederātus -a -um — federated, allied

foedītās -ātis *f*	ugliness, shame	funditus *adv*	to the bottom, utterly
foedus -a -um	ugly, hideous, shameful	fundus -ī *m*	bottom
foedus -eris *n*	treaty	fūnestus -a -um	grievous, sinister
folium -ī *n*	leaf	fungī fūnctum +*abl*	discharge, complete
fōns fontis *m*	spring, source	vītā fungī	die
forās *adv*	out	fūnis -is *m*	rope
fore *īnf fut* < esse		fūnus -eris *n*	funeral, death
forī -ōrum *m pl*	seats (in the circus)	fūr -is *m*	thief
foris -is *f*	leaf of a door, door	furca -ae *f*	fork, forked frame
forīs *adv*	outside, out of doors	furere	be mad, rage, rave
fōrma -ae *f*	form, shape, beauty	furor -ōris *m*	madness
formīdō -inis *f*	dread, terror	fūrtum -ī *n*	theft
fōrmōsus -a -um	beautiful	futūrus -a -um (*v.* esse)	future
fōrmula -ae *f*	terms, formula	(tempus) futūrum	future
forsitan/forsan	perhaps, maybe		
fortasse	perhaps, maybe	**G**	
forte *adv*	by chance	gallus -ī *m*	cock, rooster
fortis -e	strong, brave	gaudēre gavīsum esse	be glad, be pleased
fortitūdō -inis *f*	strength, bravery	gaudium -ī *n*	joy, delight
fortuītō *adv*	by chance, fortuitously	gaza -ae *f*	treasure
fortūna -ae *f*	fortune	gemellus -ī *m*	twin
fortūnātus -a -um	fortunate	gemere -uisse -itum	groan (for)
forum -ī *n*	square	gemināre	double
fossa -ae *f*	ditch, trench	geminus -a -um	twin
fragilis -e	fragile, frail	gemitus -ūs *m*	groaning
fragmentum -ī *n*	fragment, piece	gemma -ae *f*	precious stone, jewel
fragor -ōris *m*	crash	gemmātus -a -um	set with a jewel
frangere frēgisse frāctum	break, shatter	gena -ae *f*	cheek
frāter -tris *m*	brother	gener -erī *m*	son-in-law
fraus -audis *f*	deceit, guile	generāre	beget, produce
fremere -uisse	growl	generōsus -a -um	noble
fremitus -ūs *m*	rumble, growl	genetrīx -īcis *f*	mother
frendere	gnash one's teeth	geniālis -e	marriage-, conjugal
frequēns -entis *adi*	numerous, frequent	genitor -ōris *m*	father
fretum -ī *n*	strait	gēns gentis *f*	people, race, family
frētus -e -am +*abl*	relying on, confident of	genū -ūs *n*	knee
frīgēre	be cold	genus -eris *n*	kind, sort, race, gender
frīgidus -a -um	cold, chilly, cool	genus hominum	human race, mankind
frīgus -oris *n*	cold	gerere gessisse gestum	carry, bear,carry on, do,
frōns -ondis *f*	foliage, leaves		act as, *pass* go on
frōns -ontis *f*	forehead, brow, front	gestāre	carry
frūctus -ūs *m*	produce, fruit	gignere genuisse genitum	beget, create, bear
frūgēs -um *f pl*	fruit, crops	glaciēs -ēī *f*	ice
fruī +*abl*	enjoy	gladiātor -ōris *m*	gladiator
frūmentārius -a -um	corn-	gladiātōrius -a -um	gladiatorial
frūmentum -ī *n*	corn, grain	gladius -ī *m*	sword
frūstrā	in vain	globōsus -a -um	spherical, round
frūstrārī	deceive	globus -ī *m*	globe, sphere, ball, band
fuga -ae *f*	flight	glōria -ae *f*	glory
fugāre	put to flight, rout	glōriārī	boast
fugere -iō fūgisse	run away, flee	glōriōsus -a -um	glorious, boastful
fugitīvus -a -um	runaway	gnāvus -a -um	diligent, active
fulcīre -sisse -tum	hold up, support	gracilis -e, *sup* gracillimus	slender, slim
fulgēre -sisse	flash, gleam	gracilitās -ātis *f*	slenderness, thinness
fulgor -ōris *m*	flash	gradī -ior gressum	walk, proceed
fulgur -uris *n*	flash of lightning	gradus -ūs *m*	step, degree
fulmen -inis *n*	flash of lightning	Graecus -a -um	Greek
fūmus -ī *m*	smoke	grammatica -ae *f*	grammar
funda -ae *f*	sling	grammaticus -a -um	grammatical
fundāmentum -ī *n*	foundation	grandaevus -a -um	aged
fundere fūdisse fūsum	pour, shed, rout	grandis -e	big, large
funditor -ōris *m*	slinger	grandō -inis *f*	hail

16

grātēs *f pl*	thanks
grātia -ae *f*	favor, goodwill, popularity, gratitude
grātiā (/meā) +*gen*	for the sake of
grātiam habēre +*dat*	be grateful
grātiās agere +*dat*	thank
grātificārī +*dat*	oblige, gratify
grātuītus -a -um	gratuitous, futile
grātulārī +*dat*	congratulate
grātus -a -um	pleasing, grateful
gravidus -a -um	pregnant, laden
gravis -e	heavy, grave, low
gravitās -ātis *f*	weight, gravity, dignity
gremium -ī *n*	lap
grex -egis *m*	flock, herd, band
gubernāre	steer, govern
gubernātor -ōris *m*	steersman
gurges -itis *m*	whirlpool, flood
gustāre	taste

H

habēre	have, hold, make, regard
sē habēre +*adv*	get on, be
habilis -e	fit, appropriate
habitābilis -e	inhabitable
habitāre	dwell, live, inhabit
habitus -ūs *m*	state, condition
hāc *adv*	this way
haerēre -sisse -sum	stick, cling
haesitāre	hesitate, be uncertain
hasta -ae *f*	lance
haud	not
haud-quāquam	by no means
haurīre -sisse -stum	draw, bail, drink, engulf
hebes -etis	dull, blunt
heia	ah! come on!
hendeca-syllabus -a -um	of eleven syllables
herba -ae *f*	grass, herb
hercule	by Hercules! really
hērēditārius -a -um	inherited, hereditary
hērēditās -ātis *f*	inheritance
hērēs -ēdis *m*	heir
herī	yesterday
hesternus -a -um	of yesterday
heu	o! alas!
heus	hey! hello!
hexa-meter -trī *m*	hexameter
hībern(ācul)a -ōrum *n pl*	winter camp/quarters
hībernāre	spend the winter
hībernus -a -um	winter-, of winter
hic haec hoc	this
hīc	here
hiems -mis *f*	winter
hinc	from here, hence
historia -ae *f*	account, story, history
historicus -ī *m*	historian
hodiē	today
hodiernus -a -um	today's, of today
holus -eris *n*	vegetable
homō -inis *m*	human being, person
honestās -ātis *f*	honesty, virtue
honestus -a -um	honorable, *n* virtue

honor v. honōs	
honōrāre	honor
honōrificus -a -um	honorable
honōs/honor -ōris *m*	honor, high office
hōra -ae *f*	hour
horrendus -a -um	dreadful
horrēre	bristle, stand on end, shudder (at)
horribilis -e	horrible, terrifying
horror -ōris *m*	dread, horror
hortārī	encourage, urge
hortus -ī *m*	garden
hospes -itis *m*	guest, guest-friend
hospita -ae *f*	(female) guest, stranger
hospitālis -e	hospitable, guest-
hospitium -ī *n*	guest friendship/house
hostia -ae *f*	sacrificial animal
hostīlis -e	enemy-, hostile
hostis -is *m*	enemy
hūc	here, to this place
hūmānitās -ātis *f*	human feeling, culture
hūmānus -a -um	human
humī *loc*	on the ground
humilis -e, *sup* -illimus	low, humble, lowly
humus -ī *f*	ground, earth

I

iacere -iō iēcisse iactum	throw, hurl, utter, lay
iacēre	lie
iactāre	throw, toss, hurl, utter
iactūra -ae *f*	throwing away, loss
iaculārī	throw (the javelin)
iaculum -ī *n*	throwing-spear, javelin
iam	now, already
iambus -ī *m*	iamb ($\cup$—)
iānitor -ōris *m*	doorkeeper
iānua -ae *f*	door
Iānuārius -ī (mēnsis)	January
ibi	there
ibī-dem	in the same place
īcere īcisse ictum	strike, make, conclude
-icere -iō -iēcisse -iectum	
ictus -ūs *m*	stroke, blow
īdem eadem idem	the same
identidem	repeatedly
id-eō	for that reason
idōneus -a -um	fit, suitable, capable
īdūs -uum *f pl*	the 13th/15th (of the month)
iecur -oris *n*	liver
igitur	therefore, then, so
ignārus -a -um	ignorant, unaware
ignāvia -ae *f*	idleness, cowardice
ignis -is *m*	fire
ignōbilis -e	unknown, of low birth
ignōminiōsus -a -um	disgraceful
ignōrāre	not know
ignōscere -ōvisse +*dat*	forgive
ignōtus -a -um	unknown
īlicō	at once
il-lacrimāre +*dat*	weep over
ille -a -ud	that, the one, he
illecebra -ae *f*	attraction, allurement

17

illīc	there
il-licere -iō -ēxisse -ectum	entice, attract
illinc	from there
illūc	there, thither
il-lūcēscere -lūxisse	dawn, grow light
il-lūdere	make game of, fool
illūstrāre	illuminate, make clear
illūstris -e	brilliant, illustrious
imāgō -inis *f*	picture, portrait, vision
imbēcillus -a -um	weak
im-bellis -e	unwarlike, cowardly
imber -bris *m*	rain, shower
imitārī	imitate
im-mānis -e	savage, fierce
immānitās -ātis *f*	brutality, fierceness
im-mātūrus -a -um	unripe, premature
im-memor -oris *adi* (+*gen*)	unmindful, forgetful (of)
im-mēnsus -a -um	immeasurable, endless
im-minēre +*dat*	overhang, be imminent
im-minuere	make smaller, reduce
im-miscēre: sē i. (+*dat*)	mingle, merge (into)
im-mittere	send in, send (into)
immō	no, on the contrary
im-mōbilis -e	immovable, motionless
im-molāre	sacrifice, immolate
im-mortālis -e	immortal
im-mūnis -e (+*abl*)	exempt (from), tax-free
im-pār -aris *adi*	unequal
im-partīre	give a share of, impart
im-patiēns -entis *adi*	not enduring, impatient
impatientia -ae *f*	impatience
im-pavidus -a -um	fearless
impedīmentum -ī *n*	obstacle
impedīre	impede, obstruct
impedītus -a -um	obstructed, encumbered
im-pellere	strike, drive, compel
im-pendēre +*dat*	impend, threaten
impēnsa -ae *f*	cost, expenditure
imperāre (+*dat*)	command, order, levy, requisition, rule
imperātor -ōris *m*	general, emperor
imperātōrius -a -um	of a general
im-perfectus -a -um	unfinished
imperitāre (+*dat*)	govern, be in command
imperītia -ae *f*	inexperience, ignorance
im-perītus -a -um	unskilled, ignorant
imperium -ī *n*	command, empire
im-pertīre	give a share of, impart
impetrāre	obtain (by request)
impetus -ūs *m*	onset, attack, charge
im-piger -gra -grum	active, industrious
im-pius -a -um	impious
im-plēre -ēvisse -ētum	fill, fulfill, achieve
im-plicāre -uisse -itum	enfold
im-plōrāre	beseech, implore
impluvium -ī *n*	water basin
im-pōnere	place (in/on), put
impraesentiārum	at the present moment
im-primere -pressisse -pressum	press (into), stamp, impress
im-probus -a -um	bad, wicked
im-prōvīsus -a -um	unforeseen, unexpected

ex/dē imprōvīsō	unexpectedly, suddenly
im-prūdēns -entis *adi*	unwise, incautious
im-pudēns -entis *adi*	shameless, impudent
impudentia -ae *f*	shamelessness
im-pudīcus -a -um	unchaste, immoral
im-pugnāre	attack, oppose
impulsus -ūs *m*	impact, impulse
impūne	with impunity
impūnitās -ātis *f*	impunity, licence
īmus -a -um *sup*	lowest
in *prp* +*abl*	in, on, at
prp +*acc*	into, on (to), against
in-ambulāre	walk up and down
in-animus -a -um	lifeless, inanimate
inānis -e	empty, gaping
in-audītus -a -um	unheard (of)
in-calēscere -luisse	become heated
in-cautus -a -um	incautious, unsuspecting
in-cēdere	walk, advance, occur
in-cendere -disse -ēnsum	set on fire, inflame
incendium -ī *n*	fire, conflagration
inceptum -ī *n*	undertaking, enterprise
in-certus -a -um	uncertain
in-cidere -disse	occur, present itself
in-cīdere -disse -sum	cut
in-cipere -iō coepisse coeptum	begin
in-citāre	set in motion, stir up
incitātus -a -um	fast-moving, rapid
in-clāmāre	shout (at)
in-clīnāre	turn, bend, incline
in-clūdere -sisse -sum	shut up
inclutus -a -um	famous
in-cognitus -a -um	unknown
incohāre	start work on, begin
incola -ae *m/f*	inhabitant
in-colere	inhabit
incolumis -e	unharmed, safe, intact
incolumitās -ātis *f*	safety
in-commodum -ī *n*	disadvantage, misfortune
in-conditus -a -um	unpolished, rough
in-cōnspectus -a -um	unfounded
in-cōnsultus -a -um	thoughtless, rash
in-crēdibilis -e	incredible, unbelievable
in-crepāre -uisse -itum	rattle, clash, scold
in-crēscere	grow, increase
in-cultus -a -um	uncultivated, untilled
in-cumbere -cubuisse incumbere ad/in	lie down on, apply/devote oneself to
in-currere -rrisse -rsum	rush in, make an inroad
in-cursiō -ōnis *f*	incursion, inroad
in-cūsāre	reproach, accuse
inde	from there, thence(forth)
in-demnātus -a -um	uncondemned
index -icis *m*	list, catalog
in-dicāre	make known, declare
in-dīcere	notify, declare
indicium -ī *n*	information, disclosure
indigēre	be without, lack
indignārī	resent, be indignant
indignātiō -ōnis *f*	indignation, resentment
indignitās -ātis *f*	indignity, humiliation

in-dignus -a -um	unworthy, shameful
in-doctus -a -um	ignorant
indolēs -is *f*	character, nature
in-dūcere	lead, bring (in), introduce
induere -uisse -ūtum	put on (clothes)
indūtus (+*abl*)	dressed (in)
industria -ae *f*	hard work, industry
industrius -a -um	diligent, industrious
indūtiae -ae *f pl*	armistice, truce
in-ēluctābilis -e	inescapable, inevitable
in-ermis -e	unarmed, defenceless
in-ers -ertis	inactive, idle
inertia -ae *f*	idleness, sloth
in-esse	be (in)
in-explōrātō *adv*	without reconnoitering
in-expugnābilis -e	impregnable
in-exspectātus -a -um	unexpected
īn-fāmis -e	disgraced
īn-fandus -a -um	horrible
īnfāns -antis *m/f*	little child, baby
īn-fectus -a -um	unwrought, not effected
īn-fēlīx -īcis *adi*	unlucky, unfortunate
īnfēnsus -a -um	hostile
īnferior -ius *comp*	lower, inferior
īnfernus -a -um	of the underworld
īn-ferre in-tulisse il-lātum	bring (in), cause, inflict
īnferus -a -um	lower
Īnferī -ōrum *m pl*	the underworld
īnfēstāre	make unsafe, infest
īnfēstus -a -um	unsafe, infested, hostile
īn-fīdus -a -um	faithless
īn-fīgere	fix, fasten
īnfimus -a -um *sup*	lowest, the bottom of
īnfinītus -a -um	unlimited, infinite
īnfirmāre	weaken, refute, annul
īnfirmātiō -ōnis *f*	invalidation, rebuttal
īnfirmitās -ātis *f*	weakness
īn-firmus -a -um	weak
īnfitiārī	deny
īn-flammāre	kindle, inflame
īn-flāre	inflate, puff up, elate
īn-flectere	bend, turn, inflect
īn-fluere	flow into
īn-fōrmis -e	unshapely, ugly
īnfrā *prp* +*acc, adv*	below
īn-fringere -frēgisse -frāctum	break, crush
in-gemēscere -muisse	groan, moan
ingenium -ī *n*	nature, character
ingēns -entis *adi*	huge, vast
in-grātus -a -um	ungrateful
in-gredī -ior -gressum	enter, begin, walk
in-hospitālis -e	inhospitable
in-hūmānus -a -um	inhuman
in-icere	throw/lay on, instil
in-imīcus -ī *m*	(personal) enemy
in-inimīcus -a -um	unfriendly
inīquitās -ātis *f*	unfairness
in-īquus -a -um	uneven, unfair
in-īre -eō -iisse -itum	enter (upon), begin
initium -ī *n*	beginning
iniūria -ae *f*	injustice, wrong

iniūriōsus -a -um	unjust, wrongful
in-iussū +*gen*	without orders
in-iūstus -a -um	unjust, unfair
in-nocēns -entis *adi*	innocent, blameless
innocentia -ae *f*	innocence, integrity
in-numerābilis -e	countless, innumerable
inopia -ae *f*	lack, scarcity
inquit -iunt	(he/she) says/said
inquam	I say
in-quīrere -sīvisse -sītum	inquire, make inquiries
īn-sānābilis -e	incurable
īnsānia -ae *f*	madness
īn-sānus -a -um	mad, insane
īn-satiābilis -e	insatiable
īn-sciēns -entis *adi*	not knowing, unaware
īn-scius -a -um	not knowing, unaware
īn-scrībere	write on, inscribe, entitle
īnscrīptiō -ōnis *f*	inscription, title
īn-sepultus -a -um	unburied
īn-sequī	follow, pursue
īn-sīdere -sēdisse -sessum	occupy, settle, be fixed
īn-sidēre -sēdisse	hold, occupy, be seated
īnsidiae -ārum *f pl*	ambush, plot, wiles
īnsidiārī (+*dat*)	lie in wait, lie in ambush
īnsidiātor -ōris *m*	waylayer, bandit
īnsigne -is *n*	mark, token, symbol
īnsignis -e	noted, remarkable
īn-sistere -stitisse	stand (on)
īn-solēns -entis *adi*	haughty, arrogant
īnsolentia -ae *f*	arrogance
īn-solitus -a -um	unusual, unwonted
īn-sōns -ontis *adi*	innocent
īn-spērātus -a -um	unhoped for, unexpected
īn-spicere	examine, inspect
īn-stāre	press, urge, insist
īn-staurāre	renew
īnstigāre	incite, urge
īnstīnctus -a -um	roused
īn-stituere -uisse -ūtum	set up, establish, start, appoint, train, instruct
īnstitūtum -ī *n*	practice, custom, usage
īn-struere	draw up, arrange, equip
īnstrūmentum -ī *n*	tool(s), instrument
īn-suēscere -ēvisse -ētum	become accustomed
īnsula -ae *f*	island
īn-super	in addition
īnsuper habēre	overlook, neglect
in-tāctus -a -um	untouched, uninjured
integer -gra -grum	intact, unhurt, blameless
intel-legere -lēxisse -lēctum	understand, realize
in-tendere -disse -tum	strain, direct, strive
intentiō -ōnis *f*	charge, accusation
intentus -a -um	intent, attentive
inter *prp* +*acc*	between, among, during
inter sē	(with) one another
inter-cēdere	intervene, intercede
inter-clūdere -sisse -sum	cut off, block
inter-diū	by day
inter-dum	now and then
inter-eā	meanwhile
inter-esse	be between

19

interesse +*dat* — attend, take part in
interest — it matters
inter-ficere — kill
inter-icere — place between, insert, add
interiectus — situated between
interiectīs... (*abl*) — after..., at the end of...
interim — meanwhile
inter-imere -ēmisse -ēmptum — kill
interior -ius *comp* — interior, inner (part of)
inter-īre -eō -iisse — die, perish
interitus -ūs *m* — death
inter-mittere — interrupt, discontinue
interniciō -ōnis *f* — annihilation, massacre
internus -a -um — inner, internal
inter-pellāre — interrupt
inter-pōnere — place between
inter-rēgnum -ī *n* — interval between reigns
inter-rēx -rēgis *m* — intermediary regent
inter-rogāre — ask, question
inter-rumpere — break up, cut, interrupt
inter-vāllum -ī *n* — interval, space, distance
inter-venīre (+*dat*) — turn up, occur, disturb
interventus -ūs *m* — arrival
intrā *prp* +*acc* — inside, within
intrāre — enter
intrō-dūcere — lead/bring in, introduce
intro-īre -eō -iisse -itum — go inside, enter
intuērī — look at, watch
intus *adv* — inside
in-ultus -a -um — unavenged
in-ūtilis -e — useless
in-vādere -sisse -sum — enter, attack, invade
in-validus -a -um — infirm, weak
in-vehere — import, *pass* ride in
invehī in — attack in words, inveigh
in-venīre — find, meet, devise, invent
inventiō -ōnis *f* — art of devising arguments
in-vestīgāre — inquire into, investigate
in-veterāscere -rāvisse — grow old, become fixed
in-vicem — mutually, one another
in-victus -a -um — unconquered, invincible
in-vidēre +*dat* — envy, grudge
invidia -ae *f* — envy, ill will, dislike
in-violātus -a -um — unhurt
in-vīsere — go to see
in-vīsus -a -um — odious, disliked
invītāre — invite, entertain
in-vītus -a -um — unwilling, against ...'s will
in-vius -a -um — trackless, impassable
in-vocāre — call upon, invoke
iocōsus -a -um — humorous, funny
ipse -a -um — himself, that very
īra -ae *f* — anger
īrāscī — be angry
īrātus -a -um — angry
īre eō iisse itum — go
irrītāre — excite, stimulate
ir-ritus -a -um — invalid, ineffectual
ir-ruere — rush in, charge
ir-rumpere — break, force one's way
irruptiō -ōnis *f* — violent entry, assault

is ea id — he, she, it, that
iste -a -ud — this, that (of yours)
ita — so, in such a way
ita-que — therefore
item — likewise, also
iter itineris *n* — journey, march, way
iterāre — repeat, renew
iterum — again, a second time
iubēre iussisse iussum — order, tell
iūcundus -a -um — pleasant, delightful
iūdex -icis *m* — judge
iūdicāre — judge, try, decide
iūdicātiō -ōnis *f* — point at issue
iūdicium -ī *n* — judgement, trial, court
iugālis -e — marriage-, conjugal
iūgerum -ī *n* — area of ±2500 m²
iugulāre — kill, slaughter
iugulum -ī *n* — throat
iugum -ī *n* — yoke, ridge
Iūlius -ī (mēnsis) — July
iūmentum -ī *n* — beast of burden/draught
iungere iūnxisse iūnctum — join, combine, form
iūniōrēs -um *m pl* — younger men (17-45)
Iūnius -ī (mēnsis) — June
iūrāre — swear
iūs iūris *n* — law, right, justice, court
iūre — justly, rightly
iūs iūrandum iūris -ī *n* — oath
iussū *abl* +*gen* — by order of
iussum -ī *n* — command, order
iūsta -ōrum *n pl* — the last honors
iūstitia -ae *f* — justice
iūstus -a -um — just, fair, due, proper
iuvāre iūvisse iūtum — help, delight
iuvenālis -e — youthful
iuvencus -ī *m* — young bull
iuvenīlis -e — youthful
iuvenis -is *m* — young man
iuventa -ae *f* — youth
iuventūs -ūtis *f* — youth, young men
iūxtā *prp* +*acc*, *adv* — by, next to, after, alike

K

kalendae -ārum *f pl* — the 1st (of the month)
kalendārium -ī *n* — calendar

L

labefactāre — shake, undermine
lābēs -is *f* — stain, disgrace
lābī lāpsum — slip, drop, fall
labor -ōris *m* — work, toil
labōrāre — work, take trouble, suffer
labōriōsus -a -um — hard, laborious
labrum -ī *n* — lip
labyrinthus -ī *m* — labyrinth
lac lactis *n* — milk
lacerāre — tear
lacertus -ī *m* — (upper) arm
lacessere -īvisse -ītum — challenge, provoke
lacrima -ae *f* — tear
lacrimābilis -e — mournful, pitiful
lacrimāre — shed tears, weep

lacrimōsus -a -um	tearful, sad
lacteus -a -um	milky
lacus -ūs m	lake
laedere -sisse -sum	injure, hurt
laetārī	rejoice, be glad
laetitia -ae f	joy
laetus -a -um	glad, happy
laevus -a -um	left, f the left (hand)
lambere -bisse	lick, wash
lāmentātiō -ōnis f	wailing, lamentation
lāna -ae f	wool, wool spinning
lancea -ae f	lance, spear
laniāre	tear
lapideus -a -um	of stone, stone-
lapis -idis m	stone, milestone
laqueus -ī m	loop, noose
largīrī	give generously
largītiō -ōnis f	largesse, bribery
largītor -ōris m	who gives generously
largus -a -um	generous
lascīvia -ae f	wantonness
latebra -ae f	hiding-place
later -eris m	brick
latēre	be hidden, hide
latericius -a -um	of brick
Latīnus -a -um	Latin
lātrāre	bark
latrō -ōnis m	brigand, robber
latrōcinium -ī n	robbery
latus -eris n	side, flank
lātus -a -um	broad, wide
laudāre	praise
laureātus -a -um	adorned with laurel
laurus -ī f	laurel
laus laudis f	praise, merit
lavāre lāvisse lautum	wash, bathe
laxāre	loose, untie, release
lectīca -ae f	litter, sedan
lectulus -ī m	(little) bed
lectus -ī m	bed, couch
lēctus -a -um	select, picked
lēgāre	bequeath, send, delegate
lēgātiō -ōnis f	embassy, deputation
lēgātus -ī m	envoy, lieutenant, legate
legere lēgisse lēctum	read, choose, gather
legiō -ōnis f	legion
legiōnārius -a -um	legionary
lēgitimus -a -um	legal, lawful
lembus -ī m	small boat
lēnīre	placate, appease
lēnis -e	gentle, mild
lentus -a -um	slow
leō -ōnis m	lion
levāre	lift, raise
levis -e	light, slight
lēx lēgis f	law, condition, term
lībāre	make a libation, pour
libellus -ī m	little book
libēns -entis adi	willing, glad
libenter	with pleasure, gladly
liber -brī m	book
līber -era -erum	free
līberāre	free, set free, deliver
līberātor -ōris m	deliverer, liberator
libēre: libet (+dat)	it pleases
līberī -ōrum m pl	children
lībertās -ātis f	freedom, liberty
lībertīnus -ī m	freedman
libīdō -inis f	desire, lust
lībra -ae f	balance, pound (327 g)
licentia -ae f	wantonness, licence
licēre: licet +dat	it is allowed, one may
līctor -ōris m	lictor
ligāre	bind
ligneus -a -um	wooden
lignum -ī n	wood
līlium -ī n	lily
līmen -inis n	threshold
līmes -itis m	path, track
līmus -ī m	mud
līnea -ae f	string, line
lingua -ae f	tongue, language
linquere liquisse lictum	leave
linter -tris m	small boat
līs lītis f	dispute, lawsuit
littera -ae f	letter
lītus -oris n	beach, shore
lituus -ī m	augur's staff, trumpet
loca -ōrum n pl	regions, parts
locāre	place
locuplēs -ētis adi	rich, wealthy
locuplētāre	enrich
locus -ī m (pl -a -ōrum n: v. suprā)	place, position, rank, room, opportunity
longē	far, by far
longinquitās -ātis f	remoteness
longinquus -a -um	remote
longitūdō -inis f	length
longus -a -um	long
loquī locūtum	speak, talk
lūcēre lūxisse	shine
lucerna -ae f	lamp
lucrum -ī n	profit, gain
luctārī	wrestle
lūctus -ūs m	grief, mourning
lūcus -ī m	sacred grove
lūdere -sisse -sum	play
lūdibrium -ī n	toy, laughing-stock
lūdic(er) -cra -crum	of sport, of games
lūdicrum -ī n	show
lūdus -ī m	play, game, school
lūgēre -xisse	mourn, grieve (over)
lūgubris -e	sad, grievous
lūmen -inis n	light
lūna -ae f	moon
lūnāris -e	of the moon, lunar
lupa -ae f	she-wolf
lupus -ī m	wolf
lūstrāre	irradiate, purify, survey
lūstrum -ī n	ceremony of purification
lūx lūcis f	light, daylight
luxuria -ae f	extravagance, luxury
luxuriārī	revel, live in luxury
luxus -ūs m	extravagance, luxury

māceria -ae *f*	stone wall, garden wall
māchina -ae *f*	machine
māchinārī	devise, plot
macte virtūte (estō)	well done! bravo!
macula -ae *f*	stain, blemish
maculāre	stain, defile
maerēre	grieve
maeror -ōris *m*	grief
maestitia -ae *f*	sadness, sorrow
maestus -a -um	sad, sorrowful
magis	more
magister -trī *m*	schoolmaster, teacher
magister equitum	master of the horse
magistrātus -ūs *m*	office, magistrate
magnificentia -ae *f*	magnificence
magnificus -a -um	magnificent, splendid
magnitūdō -inis *f*	size, greatness
magnus -a -um	big, large, great
māior -ius *comp*	bigger, greater, older
māiōrēs -um *m pl*	ancestors
Māius -ī (mēnsis)	May
male *adv*	badly, ill
male-dīcere +*dat*	abuse, insult
maleficium -ī *n*	evil deed, crime
malitia -ae *f*	wickedness
mālle māluisse	prefer
malum -ī *n*	evil, trouble, harm
mālum -ī *n*	apple
malus -a -um	bad, wicked, evil
mamma -ae *f*	mummy
mānāre	flow, be wet, drip
mandāre	assign, order
mandātum -ī *n*	order
māne *indēcl n, adv*	morning, in the morning
manēre mānsisse	remain, stay
Mānēs -ium *m pl*	Manes, spirits of the dead
manifēstus -a -um	flagrant, plain
manipulus -ī *m*	maniple
mānsuētūdō -inis *f*	mildness, clemency
manus -ūs *f*	hand, power, force, troop
mare -is *n*	sea
margarīta -ae *f*	pearl
maritimus -a -um	sea-, coastal
marītus -ī *m*	husband
marmor -oris *n*	marble
marmoreus -a -um	made of marble, marble-
Mārtius -ī (mēnsis)	March
māter -tris *f*	mother
māteria -ae *f*	material, occasion
māternus -a -um	maternal
mātrimōnium -ī *n*	matrimony, marriage
mātrōna -ae *f*	married woman
mātrōnālis -e	of a married woman
mātūrāre	make haste, hurry
mātūrē	quickly, early
mātūritās -ātis *f*	ripeness, maturity
mātūrus -a -um	ripe, mature, timely, early
mausōlēum -ī *n*	mausoleum
māximē	most, especially
māximus -a -um *sup*	biggest, greatest, oldest
mecastor	by Castor!
medērī +*dat*	heal, cure, remedy
medicus -ī *m*	physician, doctor
mediocris -e	moderate, ordinary
meditārī	think about, contemplate
meditātiō -ōnis *f*	reflection, practicing
medium -ī *n*	middle, centre
medius -a -um	mid, middle
meherc(u)le	by Hercules!
mel mellis *n*	honey
melior -ius *comp*	better
melius *adv*	better, rather
mellītus -a -um	sweet
membrum -ī *n*	limb
mementō -tōte *imp*	remember! don't forget!
mē-met	me, myself
meminisse +*gen/acc*	remember, recollect
memor -oris *adi* (+*gen*)	mindful, reminding
memorābilis -e	memorable
memorāre	mention, speak (of)
memoria -ae *f*	memory, record
m.ae trādere/mandāre	put on record
post hominum m.am	in human memory
mendum -ī *n*	mistake, error
mēns mentis *f*	mind
mēnsa -ae *f*	table
mēnsa secunda	dessert
mēnsis -is *m*	month
mentiō -ōnis *f*	mention, reference
mentīrī	lie
mercārī	buy, purchase
mercātor -ōris *m*	merchant
mercātōrius -a -um	merchant-
mercātūra -ae *f*	trade, commerce
mercātus -ūs *m*	market, fair
mercēs -ēdis *f*	wage, fee, rent
merēre/-rī	earn, deserve
bene m. dē	behave well toward
mergere -sisse -sum	dip, plunge, sink
merīdiēs -ēī *m*	midday, noon, south
meritum -ī *n*	merit
meritus -a -um	well-deserved
merum -ī *n*	neat wine
merus -a -um	pure, neat, undiluted
merx -rcis *f*	commodity, *pl* goods
metallum -ī *n*	metal
mētārī	measure off, lay out
metere —messum	reap, harvest
mētīrī mēnsum	measure
metuere -uisse	fear
metus -ūs *m*	fear
meus -a -um, *voc* mī	my, mine
micāre	flicker, flash
migrāre	move, migrate
mīles -itis *m*	soldier
mīliārium -ī *n*	milestone
mīlitāre	serve as a soldier
mīlitāris -e	military
mīlitia -ae *f*	military service
mīlitiae (*loc*)	in the field, in war
mīlle, *pl* mīlia -ium *n*	thousand
minae -ārum *f pl*	threats
minārī	threaten

minimē — by no means, not at all
minimum *adv* — very little
minimus -a -um *sup* — smallest, youngest
minister -trī *m* — servant
ministerium -ī *n* — attendance
ministra -ae *f* — female servant
minitārī — threaten
minor -us *comp* — smaller, younger
minuere -uisse -ūtum — diminish, reduce
minus -ōris *n, adv* — less
  sī minus — if not
mīrābilis -e — marvelous, wonderful
mīrābundus -a -um — wondering
mīrāculum -ī *n* — marvel
mīrārī — wonder (at), be surprised
mīrus -a -um — surprising, strange
miscēre -uisse mixtum — mix, mix up, stir up
misellus -a -um — poor, wretched
miser -era -erum — unhappy, miserable
miserābilis -e — pitiable
miserārī — feel sorry for, pity
miserātiō -ōnis *f* — compassion, pity
miserērī +*gen* — feel pity for
miseria -ae *f* — misfortune, misery
misericordia -ae *f* — compassion, pity
missile -is *n* — missile
mītigāre — soothe
mītis -e — gentle, mild, tame
mittere mīsisse missum — send, throw
moderārī — temper, moderate
moderātiō -ōnis *f* — moderation, restraint
moderātor -ōris *m* — ruler
moderātus -a -um — restrained, moderate
modestia -ae *f* — restraint
modestus -a -um — restrained, modest
modicus -a -um — moderate
modius -ī *m* — peck (8,75 l)
modo — only, just
  modo... modo — now... now
modus -ī *m* — manner, way, measure, size, amount, limit
  nūllō modō — by no means
  huius/eius modī — of this/that kind
moenia -ium *n pl* — walls
mōlēs -is *f* — mass, bulk, effort
molestus -a -um — troublesome
  molestē patī/ferre — be annoyed (at)
mōlīrī — labor, strive
mollīre — make soft, soften
mollis -e — soft
mōmentum -ī *n* — moment
monēre — remind, advise, warn
monitus -ūs *m* — advice, prompting
mōns montis *m* — mountain
mōnstrāre — point out, show
mōnstrum -ī *n* — monster
monumentum -ī *n* — memorial, monument
mora -ae *f* — delay
morārī — delay, stay, stop
morbus -ī *m* — disease, illness
mordēre momordisse -sum — bite
morī mortuum — die

moribundus -a -um — dying
mors mortis *f* — death
mortālis -e — mortal, human
mortuus -a -um (< morī) — dead
mōs mōris *m* — custom, usage, manner
mōtus -ūs *m* — movement, rising
movēre mōvisse -tum — move, stir, ponder
mox — soon
mūgīre — low, bellow
muliebris -e — of a woman
mulier -eris *f* — woman
multāre — punish
multī -ae -a — many, a great many
multitūdō -inis *f* — large number, multitude
multō +*comp/sup* — much, by far
multum -ī *n, adv* — much, a good deal
  multum diēī — late in the day
multus -a -um — much, a good deal of
  in/ad multam noctem — till late in the night
mundus -ī *m* — world, universe
mundus -a -um — clean, neat
mūnīmentum -ī *n* — fortification
mūnīre — fortify, guard, construct
mūnītiō -ōnis *f* — fortification
mūnītus -a -um — well fortified, secure
mūnus -eris *n* — gift, task, duty
murmur -uris *n* — mutter, murmur
mūrus -ī *m* — wall
mūs mūris *m* — mouse
Mūsa -ae *f* — Muse
mūtābilis -e — changeable
mūtāre — change, exchange
mūtātiō -ōnis *f* — change
mūtus -a -um — dumb
mūtuus -a -um — on loan
  mūtuum dare/sūmere — lend/borrow

N
nam — for
-nam — ... ever?
namque — for
nancīscī nactum — get, obtain, find, meet
nāre — swim
nārrāre — relate, tell
nārrātiō -ōnis *f* — narrative
nāscī nātum — be born
nāsus -ī *m* — nose
nāta -ae *f* — daughter
natāre — swim
nātiō -ōnis *f* — people, nation
nātū *abl:* māior/minor n. — older/younger
nātūra -ae *f* — nature
nātūrālis -e — natural, of nature
nātus -a -um (< nāscī) — born
  XX annōs nātus — 20 years old
nātus -ī *m* — son
naufragium -ī *n* — shipwreck
nauta -ae *m* — sailor
nauticus -a -um — nautical, naval
nāvālia -ium *n pl* — dockyard
nāvālis -e — naval
nāvicula -ae *f* — boat

23

nāviculārius -ī *m*	shipowner
nāvigāre	sail
nāvigātiō -ōnis *f*	sailing, voyage
nāvis -is *f*	ship
-ne	...? if, whether
nē	that not, lest, that
nē... quidem	not even
nē multa	to be brief, in short
nebula -ae *f*	mist, fog
nec *v.* ne-que/nec	
necāre	kill
nec-/neque-dum	and (/but) not yet
necessārius -a-um, *adv* -ō	necessary
necessārius -ī *m*	relative, friend
necesse est	it is necessary, one must
necessitās -ātis *f*	need, necessity
nectere -x(u)isse -xum	attach
ne-fandus -a -um	heinous
ne-fās *indēcl n*	impious act, crime
ne-fāstus -a -um: diēs n.	public holiday
negāre	deny, say that... not
negitāre	deny repeatedly
neglegēns -entis *adi*	careless
neglegere -ēxisse -ctum	neglect, disregard
negōtiārī	do business, trade
negōtiātor -ōris *m*	trader
negōtium -ī *n*	business, activity, affair
nēmō, *acc* -inem, *dat* -inī	no one, nobody
nepōs -ōtis *m*	grandson
nēquam *adi indēcl* *sup* nēquissimus	worthless, bad
nē-quāquam	by no means, not at all
ne-que/nec	and/but not, nor, not
n. ... n.	neither... nor
nē-quīquam	to no effect, in vain
ne-quīre -eō -īvisse	be unable to
nervus -ī *m*	sinew, muscle
nescio-quis	someone or other, some
ne-scīre	not know
neu *v.* nē-ve/neu	
neuter -tra -trum	neither
nē-ve/neu	and (that) not, nor
n. ... n.	(that) neither... nor
nex necis *f*	killing, murder
nī *v.* nisi	
nīdus -ī *m*	nest
niger -gra -grum	black
nihil/nīl	nothing, *adv* not at all
nihilō +*comp*	no, by no means
nihilō minus/sētius	none the less
nimbus -ī *m*	rain-cloud
nī-mīrum *adv*	without doubt, evidently
nimis	too, too much
nimium -ī *n, adv*	too much, too
nimius -a -um	too big
nisi/nī	if not, except, but
nītī nīsum	exert oneself, strive
nītī in	depend on
niveus -a -um	snow-white
nix nivis *f*	snow
nōbilis -e	well known, famous
nōbilitāre	make famous
nōbilitās -ātis *f*	renown, nobility, nobles
nocēre +*dat*	harm, hurt
noctū	by night, at night
nocturnus -a -um	nocturnal, at night
nōdus -ī *m*	knot
nōlī -īte *imp* (< nōlle) +*īnf*	don't...!
nōlle nōluisse	be unwilling, not want
nōmen -inis *n*	name, fame, nation
nōmen dare	offer oneself, enroll
nōmināre	name, call
nōn	not
nōnae -ārum *f pl*	5th/7th (of the month)
nōnāgēsimus -a -um	ninetieth
nōnāgintā	ninety
nōn-dum	not yet
nōn-gentī -ae -a	nine hundred
nōn-ne	not?
nōn-nihil	not a little, something
nōn-nūllī -ae -a	some, several
nōn-numquam	sometimes
nōnus -a -um	ninth
nōs nōbīs	we, us, ourselves
nōscere nōvisse	get to know, *perf* know
nōscitāre	recognize
noster -tra -trum	our, ours
nostrum *gen*	of us
nota -ae *f*	mark, sign, slur
notāre	mark, note, censure
Notus -ī *m*	south wind
nōtus -a -um	known
novellus -a -um	new, young
novem	nine
November -bris (mēnsis)	November
nōvisse (< nōscere)	know
novissimē	quite recently
novissimus -a -um	last
novitās -ātis *f*	novelty, inexperience
novus -a -um	new, inexperienced
nox noctis *f*	night
noxa -ae *f*	harm, guilt
noxius -a -um	guilty
nūbere -psisse +*dat*	marry
nuptum dare	give in marriage
nūbēs -is *f*	cloud
nūbilus -a -um	cloudy
nūdāre	bare, leave unprotected
nūdus -a -um	naked, bare, unarmed
nūgae -ārum *f pl*	idle talk, rubbish
nūllus -a -um	no
num	...? if, whether
nūmen -inis *n*	divine will
numerāre	count
numerōsus -a -um	numerous, many
numerus -ī *m*	number, class
nummus -ī *m*	coin, sesterce
numquam	never
nunc	now
nūncupāre	designate, call
nūntia -ae *f*	messenger
nūntiāre	announce, report
nūntius -ī *m*	messenger, message
nūper	recently

nupta -ae *f*	wife
nuptiae -ārum *f pl*	wedding
nurus -ūs *f*	daughter-in-law
nusquam	nowhere
nūtrīre	feed, suckle
nūtrīx -īcis *f*	nurse
nūtus -ūs *m*	nod, gravitation
nux nucis *f*	nut
Nympha -ae *f*	nymph

O

ō	o!
ob *prp +acc*	on account of, before
ob-dūcere	draw over (to cover)
ob-equitāre	ride up to
ob-icere	place before, expose
ob-iectāre	expose
ob-īre -eō -iisse -itum	meet, visit, go into, enter upon, set
obitus -ūs *m*	death
ob-ligāre	bind
oblīquus -a -um	slanting, indirect
oblīviō -ōnis *f*	oblivion
oblīvīscī -lītum +*gen/acc*	forget
ob-mūtēscere -tuisse	become speechless
ob-nūbere	veil, cover
ob-oedīre +*dat*	obey
ob-orīrī	spring up
ob-rēpere	creep up, steal up
ob-rigēscere -guisse	become stiff
ob-ruere -ruisse -rutum	cover up, bury, crush
obscūrāre	obscure, darken
obscūrus -a -um	dark, obscure, uncertain
ob-secundāre +*dat*	comply with, obey
ob-sequī +*dat*	comply with, obey
ob-servāre	observe, respect
obses -idis *m*	hostage
ob-sidēre -sēdisse -sessum	besiege
obsidiō -ōnis *f*	siege
ob-sistere -stitisse	resist
ob-stāre	stand in the way
obstinātus -a -um	stubborn, obstinate
ob-struere	bar, block
ob-stupēscere -puisse	be stunned/astounded
ob-surdēscere -duisse	become deaf
ob-temperāre +*dat*	obey
ob-testārī	beseech, implore
ob-tinēre -uisse -tentum	hold, gain, obtain
ob-trectāre	criticize, disparage
obtrectātiō -ōnis *f*	criticism, disparagement
ob-truncāre	slaughter, kill
obtūnsus -a -um	blunt, dull
ob-venīre	fall to the lot of
ob-viam īre (+*dat*)	(go to) meet, oppose
obvius -a -um	coming to meet
obvius esse/fierī +*dat*	meet
occāsiō -ōnis *f*	opportunity, chance
occāsus -ūs *m*	setting
occidēns -entis *m*	west
oc-cidere -disse	fall, sink, set, die, end
oc-cīdere -disse -sum	kill
occultāre	hide
occultus -a -um	hidden, secret
occupāre	occupy, take possession of
oc-currere -rrisse +*dat*	meet
oc-cursāre	run to meet
ōceanus -ī *m*	ocean
ocellus -ī *m*	(little) eye
ōcissimē *sup*	most quickly
ōcius *comp*	more quickly
octāvus -a -um	eighth
octiēs	eight times
octingentī -ae -a	eight hundred
octō	eight
Octōber -bris (mēnsis)	October
octōgēsimus -a -um	eightieth
octōgintā	eighty
oculus -ī *m*	eye
ōdisse	hate
odium -ī *n*	hatred
odor -ōris *m*	smell
of-fendere -disse -ēnsum	come upon, find
offēnsa -ae *f*	offence, resentment
offēnsiō -ōnis *f*	setback, misfortune
of-ferre ob-tulisse -lātum	offer, present
officium -ī *n*	duty, task
ōlim	once, long ago, one day
ōmen -inis *n*	omen, augury
o-mittere	abandon, leave off/out
omnīnō	altogether
omnis -e	all, every
onerāre	load
onus -eris *n*	burden, load
opācus -a -um	shady
opem -is -e *acc gen abl*	power, aid, assistance
opera -ae *f*	effort, pains, service
operam dare (ut, +*dat*)	apply oneself
operae nōn est (mihi)	(I) can't spare the time
operārius -ī *m*	labourer
operīre -uisse -rtum	cover
opēs -um *f pl*	resources, wealth, power, influence
opifex -icis *m*	workman, artisan
opīmus -a -um	rich
opīnārī	think, believe
opīniō -ōnis *f*	opinion, belief
oportēre: oportet	it is right, you should
opperīrī -ertum	wait (for), await
oppidānī -ōrum *m pl*	townspeople
oppidum -ī *n*	town
op-plēre -ēvisse -ētum	fill up, cover
op-pōnere	put in the way, oppose
opportūnitās -ātis *f*	convenience, advantage
opportūnus -a -um	convenient, exposed
op-primere -pressisse -pressum	press on, overwhelm
op-pugnāre	attack
oppugnātiō -ōnis *f*	attack, assault
optāre	wish
optimātēs -ium *m pl*	the nobles/conservatives
optimus -a -um *sup*	best, very good
opulentia -ae *f*	sumptuousness
opulentus -a -um	wealthy, powerful
opus -eris *n*	work, task

25

opus est	it is needed
ōra -ae *f*	border, coast
ōrāculum -ī *n*	oracle
ōrāre	pray, beg
ōrātiō -ōnis *f*	speech
ōrātor -ōris *m*	speaker, orator, envoy
ōrātōrius -a -um	oratorical
ōrātrīx -īcis *f*	female suppliant
orbis -is *m*	circle, orbit, sphere
orbis (terrārum)	the world
orbitās -ātis *f*	loss of children/parents
orbus -a -um	childless, orphaned
ōrdināre	arrange, regulate
ōrdīrī ōrsum	begin (to speak)
ōrdō -inis *m*	row, rank, order, class
(ex) ōrdine	in order, in sequence
oriēns -entis *m*	east
orientālis -e	eastern
orīgō -inis *f*	beginnings, origin
orīrī ortum	rise, appear, spring
ōrnāmentum -ī *n*	ornament, jewel
ōrnāre	equip, adorn
ōrnātus -a -um	ornate, distinguished
ortus -ūs *m*	rising, sunrise, origin
os ossis *n*	bone
ōs ōris *n*	mouth, face
ōscitāre	gape, yawn
ōsculārī	kiss
ōsculum -ī *n*	kiss
ostendere -disse	show, demonstrate
ostentāre	display ostentatiously
ōstiārius -ī *m*	door-keeper, porter
ōstium -ī *n*	door, entrance
ōtiōsus -a -um	leisured, idle
ōtium -ī *n*	leisure, peace
ovāre	exult, rejoice
ovis -is *f*	sheep
ōvum -ī *n*	egg

P

pābulārī	forage
pābulum -ī *n*	fodder
pācāre	subdue
pacīscī pactum	contract/stipulate for
pactō: quō pactō	how
paelex -icis *f*	concubine
paene	nearly, almost
paen-īnsula -ae *f*	peninsula
paenitēre: p.et mē (+*gen*)	I regret/repent
pāgina -ae *f*	page
palam	openly, publicly
palam facere	make generally known
pālārī	stray, be dispersed
pallēre	be pale
pallēscere -luisse	grow pale
pallidus -a -um	pale
pallium -ī *n*	cloak, mantle
palma -ae *f*	palm, hand
palpitāre	beat, throb
palūdāmentum -ī *n*	military cloak
palūs -ūdis *f*	fen, swamp
pālus -ī *m*	stake

pandere -disse passum	spread out
pānis -is *m*	bread, loaf
papae!	hey!
papāver -eris *m*	poppy
papȳrus -ī *f*	papyrus
pār paris *adi*	equal, adequate
parāre	prepare, provide, get
parātus -a -um	ready
parcere pepercisse +*dat*	spare
parēns -entis *m/f*	father,mother
parentēs -um *m pl*	parents
parere -iō peperisse -rtum	give birth to, lay, produce
pārēre (+*dat*)	obey
pariēs -etis *m*	wall (of a house)
pariter	equally, together
parricīda -ae *m*	parricide
parricīdium -ī *n*	murder of near relation
pars -rtis *f*	part, direction, party
particeps -ipis *adi* +*gen*	having a share in
partim	in part, partly
partim... partim/aliī	some... others
partīrī	share, divide, distribute
parturīre	be ready to give birth to
partus -ūs *m*	(giving) birth
parum	too little, not quite
parum-per	for a short while
parvulus -a -um	little, tiny
parvus -a -um	little, small
pāscere pāvisse pāstum	pasture, feed, feast
passer -eris *m*	sparrow
passim	far and wide,everywhere
passus -ūs *m*	pace (1.48 m)
pāstiō -ōnis *f*	pasturage
pāstor -ōris *m*	shepherd
pate-facere	open, reveal
pate-fierī	be revealed
patēns -entis *adi*	open
pater -tris *m*	father, *pl* senators
patera -ae *f*	bowl
patēre	be open, spread
paternus -a -um	of the father, paternal
patēscere -tuisse	open
patī passum	suffer, bear, allow
aegrē/molestē patī	resent, be indignant
patiēns -entis *adi*	patient
patientia -ae *f*	forbearance, patience
patrāre	carry through
patria -ae *f*	native country/town
patricius -a -um	patrician
patrimōnium -ī *n*	patrimony, fortune
patrius -a -um	of the father, paternal
patrōcinium -ī *n*	protection, defence
patrōnus -ī *m*	patron, pleader, advocate
patruus -ī *m*	father's brother, uncle
paucī -ae -a	few, a few
paucitās -ātis *f*	small number, paucity
paulātim	little by little, gradually
paulisper	for a short time
paulō +*comp,* ante/post	a little
paululum	a little
paulum	a little, little
pauper -eris *adi*	poor

pavēre — be terrified
pavidus -a -um — terrified
pavor -ōris *m* — terror, fright
pāx pācis *f* — peace
peccāre — do wrong
peccātum -ī *n* — error, offence
pectus -oris *n* — breast
pecua -um *n pl* — farm animals
peculātus -ūs *m* — embezzlement
pecūlium -ī *n* — money given to slaves
pecūnia -ae *f* — money
pecūniōsus -a -um — wealthy
pecus -udis *f* — farm animal, sheep
pecus -oris *n* — livestock, sheep, cattle
pedes -itis *m* — foot-soldier
pedester -tris -tre — pedestrian, infantry
pēior -ius *comp* — worse
pellere pepulisse pulsum — push, drive (off)
-pellere -pulisse -pulsum
Penātēs -ium *m* — Penates, tutelary gods
pendere pependisse pēnsum — weigh, pay
pendēre pependisse — hang
penes *prp* + *acc* — in the possession of
penetrālia -ium *n pl* — the interior
penetrāre — penetrate
penitus *adv* — from within, deep, far
penna -ae *f* — feather
pēnsāre — weigh, ponder, consider
pēnsiō -ōnis *f* — payment, installment
pēnsitāre — pay
pēnsum -ī *n* — task
penta-meter -trī *m* — pentameter
pēnūria -ae *f* — scarcity, want
per *prp* + *acc* — through, by, during
per sē — by oneself, single-handed
per-agere — carry out, complete
per-agrāre — travel over
per-angustus -a -um — very narrow
per-blandus -a -um — very charming
per-brevis -e — very short
per-celer -is -e — very fast
per-cellere -ulisse -ulsum — strike (with fear)
per-cēnsēre — enumerate
perceptiō -ōnis *f* — gathering
per-contārī — inquire (about), ask
percontātiō -ōnis *f* — interrogation, question
per-currere -rrisse -rsum — run over, pass over
per-cutere -iō -cussisse -cussum — strike, hit
per-dere -didisse -ditum — destroy, ruin, waste, lose
per-domāre — subjugate
perduelliō -ōnis *f* — treason
peregrīnus -a -um — foreign, alien
perennis -e — enduring, perpetual
per-errāre — wander through
per-exiguus -a -um — very small
perfectus -a -um — perfect
per-ferre — carry, endure
per-ficere — complete, accomplish
perfidia -ae *f* — faithlessness, treachery
perfidus -a -um — faithless, treacherous

perfuga -ae *m* — deserter
per-fugere — take refuge
per-fugium -ī *n* — place of refuge, shelter
per-fundere — wet, drench, imbue, fill
per-fungī + *abl* — carry through, finish
pergere per-rēxisse — proceed, go on
per-grātus -a -um — very pleasing
per-hibēre — report, say
perīculōsus -a -um — dangerous, perilous
perīculum -ī *n* — danger, peril
per-imere -ēmisse -ēmptum — destroy, kill
periocha -ae *f* — summary
per-īre -eō -iisse — perish, be lost
peristȳlum -ī *n* — peristyle
perītus -a -um + *gen* — practiced, expert
per-iūcundus -a -um — very agreeable
per-magnus -a -um — very large
per-manēre — remain, continue
per-miscēre — mix, blend
per-mittere — allow, permit, leave
permixtiō -ōnis *f* — disturbance, chaos
per-molestus -a -um — very troublesome
per-movēre — move deeply
per-multī -ae -a — a great many
per-mūnīre — fortify thoroughly
per-mūtāre — exchange
permūtātiō -ōnis *f* — exchange
perniciēs -ēī *f* — destruction
perniciōsus -a -um — destructive, disastrous
per-ōrāre — conclude
per-paucī -ae -a — very few
per-pellere — enforce
perpetuus -a -um — continuous, permanent
per-rogāre — ask in turn
per-saepe — very often
per-sequī — follow, pursue
per-sevērāre — persist, continue
per-solvere — pay in full, fulfill
persōna -ae *f* — character, person
per-spicere — survey, recognize
per-stāre — stand firm, persist
per-suādēre -sisse + *dat* — persuade, convince
per-territus -a -um — terrified
per-timēscere -muisse — be frightened (of)
per-tinēre (ad) — relate, pertain (to)
per-turbāre — upset
per-vādere -sisse -sum — spread, pervade
per-vāstāre — devastate completely
per-venīre — get to, reach
per-volāre — move rapidly, rush, fly
pēs pedis *m* — foot
pessimus -a -um *sup* — worst
pessum dare — destroy, ruin
pesti-fer -era -erum — disastrous, pernicious
pestilentia -ae *f* — plague, pestilence
pestis -is *f* — plague, disaster
petasus -ī *m* — hat
petere -īvisse -ītum — make for, aim at, attack, seek, ask for, request
petītiō -ōnis *f* — pursuit, candidature
phalerae -ārum *f pl* — military decoration
phantasma -atis *n* — ghost, apparition

27

pharetra -ae *f*	quiver
philosophia -ae *f*	philosophy
philosophus -ī *m*	philosopher
pietās -ātis *f*	respect, devotion, piety
piger -gra -grum	lazy, torpid
pigēre: piget mē (+*gen*)	I am displeased, I regret
pignus -oris *n*	pledge
pila -ae *f*	ball
pilleus -ī *m*	felt cap
pīlum -ī *n*	spear, javelin
pingere pīnxisse pictum	paint, embroider
tabula picta	painting
pīpiāre	chirp
pīrāta -ae *m*	pirate
pīrāticus -a -um	of pirates
pirum -ī *n*	pear
piscātor -ōris *m*	fisherman
piscis -is *m*	fish
pius -a -um	dutiful, devoted, pious
placēre +*dat*	please
placidus -a -um	quiet, calm, gentle
placitus -a -um	pleasing, agreeable
plānē	plainly, clearly
plānus -a -um	plain, clear
plaudere -sisse (+*dat*)	clap, applaud
plausus -ūs *m*	applause
plēbēiī -ōrum *m pl*	plebeians
plēb(ē)s -is *f*	the (common) people
plēnus -a -um (+*gen/abl*)	full (of)
plērī-que plērae- plēra-	most, most people
plērumque *adv*	mostly
plērus-que plēra- plērum-	most (of),the greater part
plōrāre	cry
plūma -ae *f*	feather
plumbum -ī *n*	lead
plūrēs -a *comp*	more
plūrimī -ae -a *sup*	most, a great many
plūrimum -ī *n, adv*	most, very much
plūrimus -a -um	very much, a lot of
plūs plūris *n, adv*	more
pōculum -ī *n*	cup, glass
poēma -atis *n*	poem
poena -ae *f*	punishment, penalty
poenās dare	suffer punishment
poēta -ae *m/f*	poet
poēticus -a -um	poetical
pollēns -entis *adi*	strong
pollēre	be strong
pollicērī	promise
pollicitārī	promise
pollicitātiō -ōnis *f*	promise
polluere -uisse -ūtum	soil, violate, degrade
pōmērium -ī *n*	open space round town
pompa -ae *f*	ceremonial procession
pondō *indēcl*	in weight, pounds
pondus -eris *n*	weight
pōnere posuisse positum	place, put, pitch, lay down, take off, give up
positum esse (in)	be situated, lie, depend
pōns pontis *m*	bridge
pontifex -icis *m*	high priest
pontus -ī *m*	sea
populārī	ravage, plunder
populāris -e	of the people, popular
populāris -is *m*	fellow citizen
populus -ī *m*	people, nation
porcus -ī *m*	pig
por-rigere	stretch out
porrō	forward, ahead
porta -ae *f*	gate
portāre	carry
por-tendere -disse -tum	portend, presage
portentum -ī *n*	portent, prodigy
porticus -ūs *f*	portico, colonnade
portuōsus -a -um	having many harbors
portus -ūs *m*	harbor
poscere poposcisse	demand, call for
posse potuisse	be able
possessiō -ōnis *f*	possession, occupation
possidēre -sēdisse	possess, own
post *prp* +*acc, adv*	behind, after, later
post-eā	afterward, later
posteā-quam	after, since
posterī -ōrum *m pl*	descendants, posterity
posterior -ius *comp*	back-, hind-, later
posteritās -ātis *f*	future, posterity
posterus -a -um	next, following
posthāc	from now on, hereafter
postīcum -ī *n*	backdoor
post-quam	after, since
postrēmō *adv*	finally
postrēmum *adv*	for the last time
postrēmus -a -um *sup*	last
postrī-diē	on the following day
postulāre	demand, require
postulātum -ī *n*	demand
pōtāre	drink
potēns -entis *adi*	powerful, master(ing)
potentia -ae *f*	power
potestās -ātis *f*	power
pōtiō -ōnis *f*	drinking, drink
potior -ius *comp*	preferable, better
potīrī +*abl/gen*	take possession of, hold
potissimum *adv sup*	preferably, especially
potius *adv comp*	rather
prae *prp* +*abl*	before, for
praebēre	present, offer, show
prae-cēdere	go on ahead, precede
praeceps -ipitis *adi*	headlong, precipitous
praeceptum -ī *n*	instruction, order
prae-cipere	anticipate, advise, order
praccipitāre	throw/fall/rush headlong
praecipuē	especially, above all
praecipuus -a -um	outstanding, exceptional
prae-clārus -a -um	splendid, excellent
praecō -ōnis *m*	crier, announcer, herald
praeda -ae *f*	booty, prey
praedārī	plunder, loot
praedātōrius -a -um	plundering
prae-dicāre	declare
prae-dīcere	foretell, prophesy
praedictum -ī *n*	prediction, prophecy
praedium -ī *n*	estate
prae-dīves -itis *adi*	very rich

praedō -ōnis *m*	robber, pirate
prae-esse (+*dat*)	be in charge (of)
praefectus -ī *m*	prefect, commander
prae-ferre	prefer
prae-ficere	put in charge of
prae-mittere	send in advance
praemium -ī *n*	reward, prize
prae-nōmen -inis *n*	first name
prae-occupāre	preoccupy
prae-parāre	prepare
prae-pōnere (+*dat*)	put in charge of
prae-potēns -entis *adi*	very powerful
praesēns -entis *adi*	present, instant
(tempus) praesēns	present
prae-sentīre	have a presentiment of
praesertim	especially
praeses -idis *m/f*	guardian
praesidium -ī *n*	protection, aid, garrison
praestāns -antis *adi*	outstanding
prae-stāre -stitisse	furnish, fulfill, surpass
praestat	it is better
prae-sūmere	take for oneself, assume
praeter *prp* +*acc*	past, besides, except
praeter spem	contrary to expectation
praeter-eā	besides
praeter-īre	pass by, pass, pass over
praeteritus -a -um	past
(tempus) praeteritum	the past
praeter-mittere	omit, neglect, let pass
praeter-quam quod	apart from the fact that
praeter-vehī	ride/drive/sail past
prae-texta: toga p.	toga with purple border
praetextātus -a -um	wearing a toga praetexta
praetor -ōris *m*	praetor, commander
praetōrium -ī *n*	general's tent
praetōrius -a -um	of the commander
praetōrius -ī *m*	ex-praetor
praetūra -ae *f*	praetorship
praeverbium -ī *n*	prefix
prāt(ul)um -ī *n*	meadow, lawn
prāvus -a -um	faulty, wrong
precārī	pray
precēs -um *f pl*	prayers
prehendere -disse -ēnsum	grasp, seize
premere pressisse pressum	press, harass, press hard on, repress
pretiōsus -a -um	precious
pretium -ī *n*	price, value, reward
prīdem	long ago
prī-diē	the day before
prīmō *adv*	at first, first
prīmōrēs -um *m pl*	leading men, front ranks
prīmum *adv*	first
quam prīmum	as soon as possible
prīmus -a -um	first
prīnceps -ipis *adi, m*	first, chief, emperor
prīncipium -ī *n*	beginning, origin, basis
prior -ius	first, former, front-
prīstinus -a -um	former, previous
prius *adv*	before
prius-quam	before
prīvātim *adv*	privately, personally
prīvātum -ī *n*	private property
prīvātus -a -um	private, holding no office
prō *prp* +*abl*	before, on, for, instead of, as, according to
prō!	o!
probāre	approve of, prove
probātus -a -um	acceptable, pleasing
probus -a -um	good, honest, proper
prō-cēdere	advance, go on, succeed
procella -ae *f*	violent wind, gale
procērus -a -um	tall, long
prō-cidere -disse	fall forward, collapse
prō-clāmāre	cry out
prō-cōnsul -is *m* (prōcōs.)	proconsul, governor
prō-creāre	engender, beget
procul	far away, far (from)
procul dubiō	without doubt
prō-cumbere -cubuisse	lean forward, bow down
prō-cūrāre	attend to, administer
prōcūrātor -ōris *m*	manager, superintendent
prō-currere -rrisse -rsum	run forward, charge
prō-dere -didisse -ditum	hand down, betray
prōd-esse prō-fuisse +*dat*	be useful, do good
prōdigium -ī *n*	prodigy
prōd-īre -eō -iisse -itum	come forward, go forth
prōditiō -ōnis *f*	betrayal
prōditor -ōris *m*	traitor
prō-dūcere	bring forth, extend
proelium -ī *n*	battle
profectō	indeed, certainly
prō-ferre	fetch, produce, extend
prō-ficere	progress, be successful
proficīscī -fectum	set out, depart
pro-fitērī -fessum	declare, offer
prō-flīgāre	defeat decisively, crush
pro-fugere	run away, flee
profugus -a -um	fleeing, *m* fugitive
pro-fundere	pour out, shed
prōgeniēs -ēī *f*	offspring, descent
prō-gnātus -a -um (+ *abl*)	born, son (of)
prō-gredī -ior -gressum	go forward, advance
prōgressiō -ōnis *f*	advance
pro-hibēre	keep off, prevent, forbid
prō-icere	throw (forward)
pro-inde (+ *imp*)	accordingly
prō-lābī	slip, overbalance
prōlēs -is *f*	offspring
prōlētāriī -ōrum *m pl*	lowest class of citizens
prōmere -mpsisse -mptum	take out
prō-minēre	project, stick out
prōmissum -ī *n*	promise
prō-mittere	promise
prō-movēre	push forward, advance
prōmptū: in p.	within reach, easy
prōmptus -a -um	prompt, keen, ready
prō-mulgāre	announce, publish
prōmunturium -ī *n*	headland, promontory
prō-nūntiāre	proclaim, announce
prōnus -a -um	leaning forward, inclined
prōpatulum -ī *n*	forecourt
prope *prp* +*acc, adv*	near, nearly
properāre	hurry

29

properē	quickly
propinquus -a -um	near, close, *m* relative
propior -ius *comp*	nearer, closer
propius *adv comp*	nearer
prō-pōnere	set up, propose
prōpositum -ī *n*	objective, point
prō-praetor -ōris *m*	propraetor
proprius -a -um	own, proper
propter *prp* +*acc, adv*	because of, near
propter-eā	therefore
prōra -ae *f*	prow
prō-scrībere	proscribe, outlaw
prō-sequī	accompany, honor
prō-silīre -uisse	spring forth
prosperus -a -um	successful, favorable
prō-spicere	look out, look ahead
prō-sternere	knock down, overthrow
prō-tegere	protect
prōtinus	at once
prō-trahere	pull out, draw out
prō-vehī -vectum	sail out
prōventus -ūs *m*	growth, crop, harvest
prō-vidēre	see to it, take care
prōvincia -ae *f*	province, charge
prō-vocāre	challenge, appeal
prōvocātiō -ōnis *f*	appeal
prō-volāre	rush forth
proximus -a -um *sup*	nearest, next
proximus -ī *m*	close relative
prūdēns -entis *adi*	prudent, clever
prūdentia -ae *f*	intelligence, proficiency
pruīna -ae *f*	hoarfrost, rime
pūbēs -eris *adi*	mature, grown-up
pūblicānus -ī *m*	tax-gatherer, publican
pūblicāre	confiscate
pūblicum -ī *n*	public funds
pūblicus -a -um	public, state-
rēs pūblica	affairs of state, the state
pudēns -entis *adi*	modest, virtuous
pudēre: pudet mē (+ *gen*)	I am ashamed (of)
pudibundus -a -um	shamefaced
pudīcitia -ae *f*	chastity, virtue
pudīcus -a -um	chaste
pudor -ōris *m*	shame, decency
puella -ae *f*	girl
puer -erī *m*	boy, slave, *pl* children
puerīlis -e	of children
pueritia -ae *f*	boyhood
puerulus -ī *m*	small boy
pugna -ae *f*	fight
pugnāre	fight
pugnātor -ōris *m*	fighter, combatant
pugnus -ī *m*	fist
pulcher -chra -chrum	beautiful, fine
pulchritūdō -inis *f*	beauty
pullus -ī *m*	young one, chicken
pullus -a -um	somber, grey
pulmō -ōnis *m*	lung
pulsāre	strike, hit, knock (at)
pulsus -ūs *m*	thrust, impulse
pulvīnar -āris *n*	couch for the gods
pulvis -eris *m*	dust
pūnctum -ī *n*	dot, point, speck
pūnīre	punish
puppis -is *f, acc* -im, *abl* -ī	stern, poop
pūrgāre	clean, purge, excuse
purpura -ae *f*	purple
pūrus -a -um	clean, pure
putāre	think, suppose

Q

quā	which way, where
(sī/nē/num) quā	by any road, anywhere
quā-cumque	wherever
quadrāgēsimus -a -um	fortieth
quadrāgintā	forty
quadrātus -a -um	square
quadriennium -ī *n*	four years
quadrīgae -ārum *f pl*	team of four horses
quadringentēsimus -a -um	four hundredth
quadringentī -ae -a	four hundred
quaerere -sīvisse -sītum	look for, seek, ask (for)
quaesō	I ask you, please
quaestiō -ōnis *f*	inquiry, question
quaestor -ōris *m*	quaestor
quaestōrius -a -um	fit to be a quaestor
quaestūra -ae *f*	quaestorship
quaestus -ūs *m*	income, profit
quālis -e	what sort of, (such) as
quālis-cumque	of whatever sort
quālitās -ātis *f*	quality
quam	how, as, than
quam +*sup*	as... as possible
quam-diū	how long, (as long) as
quam-ob-rem	why
quamquam	although
quam-vīs	however, although
quandō	when, seeing that
(sī/nē/num) quandō	at any time, ever
quantitās -ātis *f*	quantity, size
quantō +*comp* (tantō...)	how much, the... (the...)
quantum -ī *n, adv*	how much, (as much) as
quantī *gen pretiī*	of what worth
quantus -a -um	how large, (as large) as
quantus-cumque -a- -um-	however great/much
quā-propter	why
quā-rē	why, therefore, hence
quārtum/quārtō *adv*	for the fourth time
quārtus -a -um	fourth
quārta pars	fourth, quarter
quasi	as, like, as if
quassāre	shake, damage, batter
quater	four times
quatere -iō	shake
quaternī -ae -a	four (each)
quattuor	four
quattuor-decim	fourteen
-que	and
quercus -ī *f*	oak
querēlla -ae *f*	complaint
querī questum	complain, grumble
querimōnia -ae *f*	complaint, protest
quī quae quod	who, which, he who
quī quae quod (...?)	what, which

quī qua quod (sī/nē...) — any
quia — because
quic-quam -quid v. quid-
quī-cumque quae- quod- / quid (v. quis) — whoever, whatever, any what, anything
quid *adv* — why
quī-dam quae- quod-/quid- quidem — a certain, some(one)
— indeed, certainly
nē quidem — not even
quidnī — why not
quid-quam/quic-quam — anything
quid-quid/quic-quid — whatever, anything that
quiēs -ētis *f* — rest, repose, sleep
quiēscere -ēvisse — rest
quiētus -a -um — quiet
quī-libet quae- quod- — no matter what/which
quīn — why not, do...! come!
quīn (etiam) — indeed, even
(nōn...) quīn +*coni* — (but) that
quī-nam v. quis-nam
quīn-decim — fifteen
quīndecim-virī -ōrum *m pl* — board of fifteen priests
quīngentēsimus -a -um — five hundredth
quīn-gentī -ae -a — five hundred
quīnī -ae -a — five (each)
quīnquāgēsimus -a -um — fiftieth
quīnquāgintā — fifty
quīnque — five
quīnquennium -ī *n* — five years
quīnque-rēmis (nāvis) — having five banks of oars
quīnquiēs — five times
Quīntīlis -is (mēnsis) — July
quīntum/quīntō *adv* — for the fifth time
quīntus -a -um — fifth
quippe (quī/quae) — inasmuch as, for
quīre -eō -īvisse — be able to
Quirītēs -ium *m pl* — Roman citizens
quis quae quid — who, what
quis quid (sī/num/nē...) — anyone, anything
quis-nam (quī-) quid-nam — who/what ever?
quis-quam — anyone
quis-que quae- quod- — each
quis-quis — anyone who, whoever
quī-vīs quae- quod- — no matter what, any
quō *adv* — where (to)
quō +*comp* (eō...) — the... (the...)
quō +*coni* — in order that (thereby)
quo-ad — until
quō-circā — hence, therefore
quō-cumque *adv* — wherever
quod (= quia) — because, that
quod sī — if however, but if
quod *n* — what, which, that which
quō-modo — how
quondam — once, some day
quoniam — since, seeing that, as
quoque — also, too
quot *indēcl* — how many, (as many) as
quot-annīs — every year
quotiēs — how often, as often as
quotiēs-cumque — every time that
quo-ūsque — how long? till when?

R

rabiēs -ēī *f* — rage, fury
radius -ī *m* — ray
rādīx -īcis *f* — root, foot, base
rāmus -ī *m* — branch, bough
rapere -iō -uisse -ptum — carry off, *pass* rush off
rapidus -a -um — rushing, rapid
rapīna -ae *f* — carrying off, plunder
raptim — hurriedly
rārō *adv* — rarely, seldom
rārus -a -um — rare
ratiō -ōnis *f* — account, consideration, reason, method, affair
ratiōnem habēre +*gen* — take into account
ratiōnālis -e — of reasoning
ratis -is *f* — raft
ratus -a -um — valid, fixed, certain
prō ratā parte — in proportion
re-bellāre — reopen the war, revolt
re-cēdere — go back, retire
recēns -entis *adi* — fresh
re-cidere reccidisse — fall back
re-cīdere -disse -sum — cut off, remove
reciperāre — recover, recapture
re-cipere — receive, admit, accept
sē recipere — retire, return, recover
recitāre — read aloud
re-cognōscere — recognize
re-conciliāre — win back, reconcile
re-cordārī — call to mind, recollect
recordātiō -ōnis *f* — recollection
re-creāre — restore, revive
rēctor -ōris *m* — ruler, governor
rēctus -a -um — straight, direct, straightforward, right, correct
rēctā (viā) — straight
re-cumbere -cubuisse — lie down
re-cūsāre — reject, refuse
red-dere -didisse -ditum — give back, render
red-igere -ēgisse -āctum — drive back, bring, reduce
red-imere -ēmisse -ēmptum — ransom
redimīre — encircle, surround
red-īre -eō -iisse -itum — go back, return
ad sē redīre — return to one's senses
reditus -ūs *m* — return
re-dūcere — lead back, bring back
red-undāre — overflow, be exuberant
re-fellere -lisse — refute
re-ferre rettulisse re-lātum — bring back, return, report, enter, refer
referre (dē) — make a proposal
rē-ferre: rē-fert (meā) — it is important (for me)
re-ficere — restore, repair
re-fugere — flee back, escape, recoil
rēgālis -e — royal
regere rēxisse rēctum — direct, guide, govern
rēgia -ae *f* — royal palace
rēgīna -ae *f* — queen
regiō -ōnis *f* — region, district
rēgius -a -um — royal
rēgnāre — reign, rule
rēgnum -ī *n* — kingship, kingdom, reign

31

re-gredī -ior -gressum	go back, return
rēgula -ae f	ruler
rēgulus -ī m	petty king, prince
re-laxāre	relax, relieve
religiō -ōnis f	fear of the gods, religion
religiōsus -a -um	sacred
re-linquere	leave
reliquiae -ārum f pl	remnants, remains
reliquum -ī n	remainder, future
reliquus -a -um	remaining, left
re-mandāre	send back word
re-manēre	remain, stay behind
remedium -ī n	remedy
rēmex -igis m	oarsman, rower
rēmigāre	row
re-mīniscī +gen/acc	recollect
remissiō -ōnis f	relaxation
remissus -a -um	gentle, relaxed
re-mittere	send back, relax
re-morārī	delay
remōtus -a -um	remote, distant
re-movēre	remove
rēmus -ī m	oar
re-nāscī	be reborn, be re-created
re-novāre	renew, resume
re-nūntiāre	report, renounce
re-parāre	repair, restore, renew
re-pellere reppulisse -pulsum	drive back, repel, rebuff
repēns -entis adi	sudden, unexpected
repente adv	suddenly
repentīnus -a -um	sudden
rēpere -psisse -ptum	crawl
reperīre repperisse repertum	find, discover, devise, invent
re-petere	return to, repeat, claim back, recall
rēs repetere	claim return of property
re-pōnere	put back
re-portāre	carry back, bring home
re-prehendere	blame, censure
re-primere -essisse -essum	check, repress, restrain
repudiāre	reject, refuse to accept
re-pugnāre	fight back, resist
repulsa -ae f	defeat (in an election)
re-putāre	think over, reflect on
re-quiēscere	rest
re-quīrere -sīvisse -sītum	seek, ask
rērī ratum	reckon, think, believe
rēs reī f	thing, matter, affair
rēs (pūblica)	affairs of state, the state
re-scindere	demolish, cancel, annul
re-sīdere -sēdisse	sink back, subside
re-sistere -stitisse +dat	halt, resist
re-sonāre	resound
re-spergere -sisse -sum	sprinkle, splatter
re-spicere	look back (at), heed, regard, have regard for
re-spondēre -disse -sum	answer
respōnsum -ī n	answer
re-stāre -stitisse	remain, be left
restat (ut)	it remains

re-stinguere -stīnxisse -stīnctum	put out, extinguish
restis -is f	rope
re-stituere -uisse -ūtum	rebuild, restore, reinstate
re-surgere	rise again, be restored
re-tardāre	delay, hold up
rēte -is n	net
re-ticēre	keep silent
re-tinēre -uisse -tentum	hold back
re-trahere	pull back, bring back
retrō	back
reus -ī m	defendant, accused
re-vehere	bring back
re-venīre	come back
revertī -tisse -sum	return, come back
re-vincere	conquer
re-vīsere	revisit, visit
re-vocāre	call back, recall, revoke
rēx rēgis m	king
rhētor -oris m	teacher of rhetoric
rīdēre -sisse -sum	laugh, make fun of
rīdiculus -a -um	ridiculous
rigāre	irrigate
rigēre	be stiff
rīpa -ae f	bank
-ripere -iō -uisse -reptum	
rīsus -ūs m	laughter, laugh
rīte adv	with due rites, properly
rītus -ūs m	rites, ceremonies
rīvus -ī m	brook, channel
rixa -ae f	quarrel, brawl
rōbur -oris n	oak, strength, force
rōbustus -a -um	strong, robust
rogāre	ask, ask for
rogātiō -ōnis f	proposed law, bill
rogitāre	ask (repeatedly)
rogus -ī m	funeral pyre
Rōmānus -a -um	Roman
rosa -ae f	rose
rōstra -ōrum n pl	speakers' platform
rōstrātus -a -um	having a beaked prow
rōstrum -ī n	beak, beaked prow
rota -ae f	wheel
rotundus -a -um	round
ruber -bra -brum	red
rubēre	be red, blush
rudis -e	crude, rude
ruere ruisse	rush, tumble down
ruīna -ae f	collapse, ruin
rūmor -ōris m	rumor
rumpere rūpisse ruptum	burst, break, break off
rūpēs -is f	crag, rock
ruptor -ōris m	one who breaks
rūrī loc	in the country
rūrsus adv	again
rūs rūris n	the country
rūsticus -a -um	rural, rustic, farm-
rutilus -a -um	red
S	
sacculus -ī m	purse
saccus -ī m	sack

sacer -cra -crum	holy, sacred
sacerdōs -ōtis m/f	priest, priestess
sacrāre	consecrate
sacrārium -ī n	sanctuary
sacrificāre	make a sacrifice
sacrificium -ī n	sacrifice
sacrum -ī n	sacred object, sacrifice
saeculum -ī n	generation, age, century
saepe -ius -issimē	often
saepīre	surround
saevitia -ae f	savageness, cruelty
saevus -a -um	fierce, cruel
sagitta -ae f	arrow
sagittārius -ī m	archer, bowman
sāl salis m	salt, wit
salīnae -ārum f pl	salt-pans,
salīre -uisse	jump
saltāre	dance
saltem	at least, anyhow
saltus -ūs m	wooded hills
salūber -bris -bre	healthy, salutary
salūs -ūtis f	health, salvation, safety
salūtem dīcere +dat	greet
salūtāre	greet
salūtāris -e	wholesome, salutary
salvāre	save
salvē -ēte	hallo, good morning
salvēre iubēre	greet
salvus -a -um	safe, unharmed
sānāre	heal, cure
sānctus -a -um	holy
sānē	certainly, quite
sanguineus -a -um	blood-stained, bloodshot
sanguinulentus -a -um	blood-stained
sanguis -inis m	blood, race, relationship
sānus -a -um	healthy, well
sapere -iō -iisse	be wise, have sense
sapiēns -entis adi	wise
sapientia -ae f	wisdom
sarcina -ae f	pack, kit
sarmentum -ī n	brushwood, branch
satelles -itis m	henchman, attendant
satis	enough, rather
satius comp < satis	better, preferable
saucius -a -um	wounded
saxum -ī n	rock
scaena -ae f	scene, stage
scaenicus -a -um	theatrical
scālae -ārum f pl	ladder
scalpellum -ī n	scalpel, surgical knife
scamnum -ī n	stool
scandere -disse -ānsum	climb, mount
scelerātus -a -um	accursed, criminal
scelestus -a -um	criminal, wicked
scelus -eris n	crime
scēptrum -ī n	sceptre
sciēns -entis adi +gen	having knowledge of
scientia -ae f	knowledge
scīlicet	of course
scindere -idisse -issum	tear, tear up
scīre	know
scīscitārī	inquire, ask
scopulus -ī m	rock
scortum -ī n	prostitute, whore
scrībere -psisse -ptum	write, describe, enroll
scrīptor -ōris m	writer
scrīptum -ī n	writing, book
scrīptūra -ae f	tax on grazing rights
scrūtārī	examine, search
scūtum -ī n	shield
sē/sēsē acc/abl, dat sibi	himself, each other
secāre -uisse -ctum	cut
sē-cernere	separate, detach
sēcrētō adv	in private
sēcrētum -ī n	seclusion, privacy
secundō adv	for the second time
secundum prp +acc	along, after, according to
secundus -a -um	second, favorable
secūris -is f, acc -im, abl -ī	axe
secus adv	otherwise
sed	but
sēdāre	allay, appease, calm
sē-decim	sixteen
sedēre sēdisse	sit
sēdēs -is f	seat, abode, dwelling
sēditiō -ōnis f	discord, insurrection
sēditiōsus -a -um	seditious
sēgnis -e	slothful, inactive
sē-iungere	separate
sella -ae f	stool, chair
semel	once
sēmen -inis n	seed, offspring
sē-met	himself, themselves
sēmi-animis -e	half-alive
sēmi-ermis -e	half-armed
sēmi-somnus -a -um	half-asleep
semper	always
sempiternus -a -um	everlasting, eternal
senātor -ōris m	senator
senātus -ūs m	senate, assembly, sitting
senecta -ae f	old age
senectūs -ūtis f	old age
senēscere -nuisse	grow old, weaken
senex senis m	old man
sēnī -ae -a	six (each)
senior -ōris comp	older
sēnsim	gradually, little by little
sēnsus -ūs m	sense, sensation
sententia -ae f	opinion, sentence
sentīre sēnsisse -sum	feel, sense, think
sepelīre -īvisse -ultum	bury
septem	seven
September -bris (mēnsis)	September
septen-decim	seventeen
septēnī -ae -a	seven (each)
septentriōnālis -e	northern
septentriōnēs -um m pl	north
septimus -a -um	seventh
septingentēsimus -a -um	seven hundredth
septin-gentī -ae -a	seven hundred
septuāgēsimus -a -um	seventieth
septuāgintā	seventy
sepulcrum -ī n	tomb, grave
sequī secūtum	follow

serēnus -a -um — clear, cloudless, calm
serere sēvisse satum — sow, plant
sērius *comp adv* < sērō — later, too late
sērius -a -um — serious
sermō -ōnis *m* — talk, language
serō *adv, comp* sērius — late
serpēns -entis *m* — snake, serpent
sērus -a -um — late
serva -ae *f* — female slave
servāre — preserve, save
servātor -ōris *m* — savior
servīlis -e — of a slave, servile
servīre +*dat* — be a slave, serve
servitium -ī *n* — slavery
servitūs -ūtis *f* — slavery
servus -ī *m* — slave, servant
sescentēsimus -a -um — six hundredth
ses-centī -ae -a — six hundred
sēsē *v.* sē
sēstertius -ī *m* — sesterce (coin)
sētius: nihilō sētius — none the less
seu *v.* sī-ve/seu
sevērus -a -um — stern, severe
sex — six
sexāgēsimus -a -um — sixtieth
sexāgintā — sixty
sexiēs — six times
Sextīlis -is (mēnsis) — August
sextus -a -um — sixth
sī — if
sīc — in this way, so, thus
siccāre — dry, drain
siccus -a -um — dry
sīc-ut/-utī — just as, as
sīdere sēdisse sessum — sit down, settle
sīdus -eris *n* — star, heavenly body
signāre — mark, seal, stamp
significāre — indicate, mean
significātiō -ōnis *f* — intimation, meaning
signum -ī *n* — sign, seal, signal, statue, ensign
silentium -ī *n* — silence
silēre — be silent
silva -ae *f* — wood, forest
silvestris -e — of the woods, wild
similis -e (+*gen/dat*), *sup* -illimus — similar, like
vērī similis — probable, convincing
simplex -icis *adi* — simple, single, plain
simul — together, at the same time
simul (atque) +*perf* — as soon as
simulācrum -ī *n* — image, statue
simulāre — pretend
simultās -ātis *f* — enmity, quarrel
sīn — but if
sine *prp* +*abl* — without
sinere sīvisse situm — let, allow
singulāris -e — single, singular, unique
singulī -ae -a — one (each), each
sinister -tra -trum — left, *f* the left (hand)
sinus -ūs *m* — bay, fold (of toga), breast
sī-quidem — seeing that, since

sistere — halt, stop
sitīre — be thirsty
sitis -is *f* — thirst
situs -a -um — situated, based, dependent
situs -ūs *m* — position, situation
sī-ve/seu — or, or if
s. ... s. — whether... or
socer -erī *m* — father-in-law
sociālis -e — of allies, social
sociāre — join, unite
societās -ātis *f* — partnership, alliance
socius -ī *m* — companion, partner, ally
socordia -ae *f* — sluggishness, indolence
sōl -is *m* — sun
sōlārī — comfort
solēre -itum esse — be accustomed
sōlitūdō -inis *f* — loneliness, lonely place
solitus -a -um — usual
solium -ī *n* — throne
sollicitāre — solicit, incite
solum -ī *n* — soil, ground, floor
sōlum *adv* — only
sōlus -a -um — alone, lonely
solūtus -a -um: ōrātiō s.a — prose
solvere -visse solūtum — untie, loosen, dissolve, abolish, discharge, pay
nāvem solvere — cast off, set sail
somnium -ī *n* — dream
somnus -ī *m* — sleep
sonāre -uisse — sound
sonitus -ūs *m* — noise, sound
sonus -ī *m* — sound
sōpīre — cause to sleep, stun
sōpītus — sleeping, asleep
sordēs -ium *f pl* — dirt
sordidus -a -um — dirty, mean, base
soror -ōris *f* — sister
sors -rtis *f* — lot, drawing lots, fortune
sortīrī — draw lots
sōspes -itis *adi* — safe and sound
spargere -sisse -sum — scatter
spatium -ī *n* — space, distance, interval, walk, time, period
speciēs -ēī *f* — sight, appearance, shape, semblance, sort, species
spectāculum -ī *n* — sight, spectacle, *pl* seats
spectāre — watch, look at
spectāre ad — face, tend to, aim at
spectātor -ōris *m* — spectator
spectātus -a -um — manifest, undisputed
speculārī — spy, reconnoiter
speculātor -ōris *m* — scout, spy
speculum -ī *n* — mirror
specus -ūs *m* — cave, grotto
spēlunca -ae *f* — cave, grotto
spērāre — hope (for)
spernere sprēvisse -ētum — disdain, scorn
spēs -eī *f* — hope
sphaera -ae *f* — globe, sphere
-spicere -iō -spexisse -spectum
spīrāre — breathe, blow

34

splendēre	shine
splendidus -a -um	shining, splendid
splendor -ōris m	brightness, splendor
spolia -ōrum n pl	spoils, booty
spoliāre	strip (of arms), rob
spondēre spopondisse spōnsum	pledge, promise, betroth
spondēus -ī m	spondee (——)
spōnsus -ī m	fiancé
sponte (meā/suā)	of my/his own accord
stabilis -e	firm, stable
stabulum -ī n	stable
stadium -ī n	running-track
stāgnum -ī n	pool, pond
stāre stetisse	stand, endure, cost
statim	at once
statiō -ōnis f	post, guard, anchorage
statīva -ōrum n pl	permanent camp
statua -ae f	statue
statuere -uisse -ūtum	fix, determine, decide
status -ūs m	state, condition, order
stēlla -ae f	star
stēllifer -era -erum	star-bearing
sterilis -e	barren, sterile
sternere strāvisse strātum	spread, knock down
viam sternere	pave a road
stīllāre	drip
stilus -ī m	stylus, writing
stimulāre	spur on, stimulate
stipendium -ī n	soldier's pay, service
stīpes -itis m	stake, stick
stirps -pis f	origin, stock, offspring
strāgēs -is f	slaughter
strāmentum -ī n	straw
strēnuus -a -um	active, vigorous
strepere -uisse	make a noise
strepitus -ūs m	noise, din
stringere -īnxisse -ictum	draw, unsheathe
strophē -ae f	verse, stanza
struere -ūxisse -ūctum	arrange, contrive, devise
studēre +dat	devote oneself to
studiōsus -a -um (+gen)	interested (in)
studium -ī n	interest, study
stultitia -ae f	stupidity, folly
stultus -a -um	stupid, foolish
stupe-factus -a -um	amazed, stupefied
stupēre	be aghast
stuprāre	violate, rape
stuprum -ī n	rape
suādēre -sisse -sum +dat	advise
sub prp +abl/acc	under, near
sub-agrestis -e	somewhat boorish
sub-dere -didisse -ditum	set (spurs to)
sub-dūcere	draw up, beach, lead off
sub-icere	put under, subject, add
sub-iectus -a -um +dat	situated under
sub-igere -ēgisse -āctum	subdue, drive, force
sub-inde	immediately afterward
sub-īre -eō -iisse -itum	go under, undergo
subitō adv	suddenly
subitus -a -um	sudden
sub-legere	appoint
sublīmis -e	high (up), aloft
sub-mergere	sink
sub-mittere	lower
sub-movēre	remove, drive off
sub-nīxus -a -um +abl	resting on, relying on
sub-scrībere	write underneath
subsellium -ī n	bench
subsidium -ī n	support, help, resource
subter adv	below, underneath
sub-terrāneus -a -um	underground
sub-urbānus -a -um	near the city
sub-venīre +dat	come to help
suc-cēdere (+dat)	enter, succeed, follow
successor -ōris m	successor
successus -ūs m	success
suc-cingere	surround
suc-clāmāre	shout in response
suc-cumbere -cubuisse +dat	yield, submit
suc-currere -rrisse +dat	(run to) help
sūdor -ōris m	sweat
suf-ficere	appoint, substitute
suffīxum -ī n	suffix
suf-frāgārī	vote for, support
suffrāgium -ī n	vote
sūmere -mpsisse -mptum	take, take up, adopt, assume
summa -ae f	total, sum, main part
summus -a -um sup	highest, greatest, top of
sūmptus -ūs m	expenditure, expense
su-ove-taurīlia -ium n pl	purificatory sacrifice
super prp +acc, adv	on , on top (of), above
prp +abl	on, about
superāre	cross, surpass, overcome, defeat, remain
superbia -ae f	arrogance, pride
superbus -a -um	haughty, proud
super-ēminēre	stand out above
super-esse	be left, be over, survive
super-fundere	pour over, spread
superior -ius comp	higher, superior, former
superus -a -um	upper
super-venīre (+dat)	appear, surprise
suppeditāre	supply
supplēmentum -ī n	reinforcement
sup-plēre -ēvisse -ētum	fill up, reinforce
supplex -icis adi	suppliant
supplicātiō -ōnis f	thanksgiving
supplicium -ī n	(capital) punishment
suprā prp +acc	above, on, over
adv	above, further back
suprēmus -a -um sup	highest, sovereign
surdus -a -um	deaf
surgere sur-rēxisse	rise, get up
sur-ripere	steal
sūrsum adv	up, upwards
sūs suis f	pig
sus-cipere	take up, receive, adopt
suscitāre	wake up, rouse
suspectus -a -um	suspected, suspect
sus-pendere -disse -ēnsum	hang, suspend
suspicārī	guess, suspect

35

su-spicere	look up (at)	tenebricōsus -a -um	dark
suspiciō -ōnis f	suspicion	tener -era -erum	tender, delicate
sustentāre	sustain, maintain, endure	tenēre -uisse -ntum	hold, keep (back), reach,
sus-tinēre -uisse -tentum	support, sustain, main-		hold one's course, sail
	tain, endure	tenuis -e	thin
suus -a -um	his/her/their (own)	ter	three times
syllaba -ae f	syllable	terere trīvisse trītum	wear out, use up, spend
synōnymum -ī n	synonym	tergēre -sisse -sum	wipe
		tergum -ī n	back
T		terminus -ī m	boundary(-stone)
tabella -ae f	(writing-)tablet	ternī -ae -a	three (each)
tabellārius -ī m	letter-carrier	terra -ae f	earth, ground, country
taberna -ae f	shop, stall	terrēre	frighten
tabernāculum -ī n	tent	terrestris -e	earthly, terrestrial
tabernārius -ī m	shopkeeper	terribilis -e	terrible
tābēscere -buisse	waste away, decay	terror -ōris m	fright, terror
tabula -ae f	(writing-)tablet, painting	tertium/tertiō adv	for the third time
tabulārium -ī n	record-office	tertius -a -um	third
tacēre	be silent (about)	testāmentum -ī n	will, testament
tacitus -a -um	silent	testārī	call to witness
taedēre: taedet mē (+gen)	I am tired/sick of	testis -is m/f	witness
taeter -tra -trum	foul, horrible	thalamus -ī m	bedroom
talentum -ī n	talent	theātrum -ī n	theater
tālis -e	such	thema -atis n	stem, theme
tam	so, as	thermae -ārum f pl	public baths
tam-diū	so long, as long	thēsaurus -ī m	treasure
tamen	nevertheless, yet	tībiae -ārum f pl	flute
tam-etsī	although	tībīcen -inis m	flute-player
tam-quam	as, like, as though	tigris -is f	tiger
tandem	at last, do...! then (...?)	timēre	fear, be afraid (of)
tangere tetigisse tāctum	touch	timidus -a -um	fearful, timid
tantum -ī n	so much	timor -ōris m	fear
tantī gen pretiī	of such worth	tingere tīnxisse tīnctum	wet, soak
alterum tantum	twice as much	tīrō -ōnis m	recruit
tantum adv	so much, only	titulus -ī m	title
tantum-modo	only, merely	toga -ae f	toga
tantun-dem	just as much	togātus -a -um	wearing the toga
tantus -a -um	so big, so great	tolerābilis -e	tolerable
tardāre	delay	tolerāre	bear, endure
tardus -a -um	slow, late	tollere sus-tulisse sub-	raise, pick up, remove,
tata -ae m	daddy	lātum	abolish, put an end to
taurus -ī m	bull	tonāre -uisse	thunder
tēctum -ī n	roof, house	tonitrus -ūs m	thunder
tēctus -a -um	covered, decked	torquātus -a -um	wearing a collar
tegere tēxisse tēctum	cover, conceal	torquis -is m	collar
tellūs -ūris f	earth	torrēre -uisse tōstum	scorch, parch
tēlum -ī n	spear, weapon	torridus -a -um	scorched, parched
temerārius -a -um	reckless	torus -ī m	bed
temere adv	heedlessly	tot indēcl	so many
temeritās -ātis f	recklessness	tot-idem indēcl	as many
temperantia -ae f	self-control, moderation	totiēs	so many times
temperāre	moderate, temper, refrain	tōtus -a -um	the whole of, all
temperātiō -ōnis f	organizing power	trabs -bis f	beam, ship
temperātus -a -um	moderate, restrained	tractāre	handle, treat, manage
tempestās -ātis f	storm, period	trā-dere -didisse -ditum	hand over, deliver, tell
tempestīvus -a -um	timely, suitable	trā-dūcere	move (across), pass
templum -ī n	temple, (sacred) space	tragicus -a -um	tragic
temptāre	try (to influence), attack	tragoedia -ae f	tragedy
tempus -oris n	time, opportunity	trāgula -ae f	spear, javelin
tendere tetendisse	stretch, spread, lay, make	trahere -āxisse -actum	drag, pull, draw, derive,
tentum/tēnsum	one's way, insist		draw out, protract
tenebrae -ārum f pl	darkness	trā-icere	take across, cross, pierce

trā-natāre	swim across
tranquillitās -ātis f	calmness
tranquillus -a -um	calm, still
trāns prp +acc	across, over, beyond
trān-scendere -disse	climb across, cross
trāns-ferre	transfer, convey, carry
trāns-fīgere	pierce
trāns-fuga -ae m	deserter
trāns-fugere	go over, desert
trāns-gredī -ior -gressum	cross
trāns-igere -ēgisse -āctum	carry through, finish
trān-silīre -uisse	jump over
trāns-īre -eō -iisse -itum	cross, pass, go over
trānsitiō -ōnis f	crossing over, defection
trānsitus -ūs m	crossing, passage
trāns-marīnus -a -um	from beyond the seas
trāns-mittere	send over, cross
trāns-portāre	carry across, transport
trāns-vehere	carry (pass sail) across
trāns-versus -a -um	placed crosswise
trecentēsimus -a -um	three hundredth
tre-centī -ae -a	three hundred
trē-decim	thirteen
tremere -uisse	tremble
trepidāre	be in panic, tremble
trepidātiō -ōnis f	alarm, panic
trepidus -a -um	alarmed, in panic
trēs tria	three
tribuere -uisse -ūtum	grant, attribute
tribūnal -ālis n	dais, platform
tribūnātus -ūs m	office of tribune
tribūnus -ī m	tribune
tribus -ūs f	tribe (division of citizens)
tribūtum -ī n	tax
trīcēsimus -a -um	thirtieth
trīclīnium -ī n	dining-room
tridēns -entis m	trident
trīduum -ī n	three days
triennium -ī n	three years
triēns -entis m	third of an as
trigeminus -a -um	triplet
trigintā	thirty
trīnī -ae -a	three
trirēmis -e	trireme
trīstis -e	sad
trīstitia -ae f	sadness
trīticum -ī n	wheat
triumphālis -e	triumphal
triumphāre	celebrate a triumph
triumphus -ī m	triumph
trium-virī -ōrum m pl	commission of three
trium-virālis -e	of the triumvirs
trochaeus -ī m	trochee (— ◡)
trucīdāre	slaughter
trux -ucis adi	savage, grim
tū tē tibi (gen tuī)	you, yourself
tuba -ae f	trumpet
tubicen -inis m	trumpeter
tuērī tūtum	guard, protect, look at
tugurium -ī n	hut
tum	then
cum... tum...	not only... but also...

tumēre	swell
tumidus -a -um	swollen
tumulōsus -a -um	hilly
tumultuārī	make an uproar
tumultuārius -a -um	casual, unplanned
tumultus -ūs m	uproar
tumulus -ī m	hillock, burial-mound
tunc	then
tunica -ae f	tunic
turba -ae f	disorder, throng, crowd
turbāre	stir up, disturb, upset
turbidus -a -um	agitated, stormy
turgid(ul)us -a -um	swollen
turma -ae f	squadron
turmātim	in squadrons
turpis -e	ugly, foul, shameful
turris -is, acc -im, abl -ī	tower
tūtārī	protect
tūtō adv	safely
tūtor -ōris m	guardian
tūtus -a -um	safe
tuus -a -um	your, yours
tyrannis -idis f	tyranny
tyrannus -ī m	tyrant

U	
ūber -eris n	udder
ūber -eris adi	fertile
ūbertās -ātis f	fruitfulness
ubi	where
ubi (prīmum) +perf	as soon as
ubi-cumque	wherever
ubī-que	everywhere
ūdus -a -um	wet
ulcīscī ultum	revenge, avenge
ūllus -a -um	any
ulterior -ius comp	farther, more distant
ultimus -a -um sup	most distant, last
ad ultimum	finally
ultor -ōris m	avenger
ultrā prp +acc, adv	beyond, further
ultrīx -īcis adi f	avenging
ultrō	spontaneously
ultrō citrō(que)	back and forth
ululāre	howl
ululātus -ūs m	howling
umbra -a f	shade, shadow
umerus -ī m	shoulder
ūmidus -a -um	wet, moist
umquam	ever
ūnā adv	together
unda -ae f	wave
unde	from where
ūn-dē-centum	ninety-nine
ūn-decim	eleven
ūndecimus -a -um	eleventh
ūn-dē-trīgintā	twenty-nine
ūn-dē-vīcēsimus -a -um	nineteenth
ūn-dē-vīgintī	nineteen
undique	from all sides
unguis -is m	nail, claw
ūnī -ae -a	one

ūnicē — particularly
ūnicus -a -um — one and only, sole
ūniversus -a -um — the whole of, entire
ūnus -a -um — one, only
ad ūnum — without exception
ūnus-quisque — each one
urbānus -a -um — of the city, urban
urbs -bis *f* — city
ūrere ussisse ustum — burn
urgēre -sisse — press, oppress
usquam — anywhere
ūsque — up (to), all the time
ūsus -ūs *m* — use, practice, usage
  ūsū venīre — occur
  ūsuī/ex ūsū esse — be of use
ut/utī — like, as, how
  ut +*coni* — that, in order that, to
  ut (prīmum) +*perf* — as soon as
ut-cumque — no matter how, however
uter utra utrum — which (of the two)
uter-que utra- utrum- — each of the two, both
utī *v.* ut
ūtī ūsum +*abl* — use, enjoy
ūtilis -e — useful
ūtilitās -ātis *f* — interest, advantage
utinam — I wish that, if only...!
utpote — namely
utrimque — on/from both sides
utrobīque — in both places
utrum... an — ... or...? whether... or
ūva -ae *f* — grape
uxor -ōris *f* — wife
uxōrius -a -um — attached to one's wife

V

vacuus -a -um — empty
vādere — advance, go
vadum -ī *n* — ford, *pl* shallows
vagārī — wander, roam
vāgīna -ae *f* — sheath
vāgīre — wail, squall
vāgītus -ūs *f* — wail, squall
vagus -a -um — wandering, roaming
valdē — strongly, very (much)
valē -ēte — farewell, goodbye
valēns -entis *adi* — strong
valēre — be strong, be well
valētūdō -inis *f* — health, illness
validus -a -um — strong
vāllāre — fortify, defend
vallis -is *f* — valley
vāllum -ī *n* — rampart
vāllus -ī *m* — stake (for a palisade)
vānus -a -um — empty, useless, vain
varietās -ātis *f* — variety, diversity
varius -a -um — varied, different
vās vāsis *n, pl* -a -ōrum — vessel, bowl
vāstāre — lay waste, ravage
vāstus -a -um — desolate, vast, huge
vātēs -is *m/f* — prophet(ess), seer
-ve — or
vectīgal -ālis *n* — (indirect) tax

vectīgālis -e — tax-paying, tributary
vehemēns -entis *adi* — violent
vehere vēxisse vectum — carry, convey, *pass* ride, sail, travel
vehiculum -ī *n* — waggon, vehicle
vel — or, even
vēlāre — cover
velle volō voluisse — want, be willing
vēlōx -ōcis *adi* — swift, rapid
vēlum -ī *n* — sail
vel-ut — like, as
vēna -ae *f* — vein
vēnālis -e — for sale
vēnārī — go hunting, hunt
vēnātor -ōris *m* — hunter
vēn-dere -didisse — sell
venēnātus -a -um — poisoned, poisonous
venēnum -ī *n* — poison
venia -ae *f* — favor, leave, pardon
venīre vēnisse ventum — come
vēn-īre -eō iisse — be sold
venter -tris *m* — belly, stomach
ventitāre — come frequently
ventus -ī *m* — wind
vēnun-dare — put up for sale
venustus -a -um — charming
vēr vēris *n* — spring
verbera -um *n pl* — lashes, flogging
verberāre — beat, flog
verbum -ī *n* — word, verb
verērī — fear
vergere — slope, point, turn
vērō — really, however, but
  neque/nec vērō — but not
versāre — turn over, ponder
versārī — turn, move about, be
versiculus -ī *m* — short verse
versus -ūs *m* — line, verse
versus: ad... *v.* — toward
vertere -tisse -sum — turn, change
vertex -icis *m* — whirlpool, peak, pole
vērum — but
vērum -ī *n* — truth
  vērī similis — probable, convincing
vērus -a -um — true, real, proper
vescī +*abl* — feed on, eat
vesper -erī *m* — evening
vesperī *adv* — in the evening
vester -tra -trum — your, yours
vestibulum -ī *n* — forecourt
vestīgium -ī *n* — footprint, trace
vestīmentum -ī *n* — garment, clothing
vestīre — dress
vestis -is *f* — clothes, cloth
vestrum *gen* — of you
vetāre — forbid
vetus -eris, *sup* -errimus — old
vetustās -ātis *f* — age
vetustus -a -um — ancient, old
vexāre — harass, trouble, ravage
vexillum -ī *n* — standard, ensign
via -ae *f* — road, way, street

viāticum -ī n — provision for a journey
vicem: in/per vicem — in turn, mutually
vīcēsimus -a -um — twentieth
vīcīnitās -ātis f — neighborhood, vicinity
vīcīnus -a -um — neighboring
vicissim — in turn
victima -ae f — victim
victor -ōris m, adi — conqueror, victorious
victōria -ae f — victory
victrīx -īcis adi f — victorious
vīcus -ī m — street, village
vidēlicet — evidently, of course
vidēre vīdisse vīsum — see, *pass* seem
vidua -ae f — widow
vigēre — be vigorous
vigil -is adi — wakeful, watchful
vigilāns -antis adi — waking, wakeful
vigilāre — be awake
vigilia -ae f — night watch, vigil
vīgintī — twenty
vigor -ōris m — vigor
vīlis -e — cheap
vīlitās -ātis f — cheapness, low price
vīlla -ae f — country house, villa
vincere vīcisse victum — defeat, overcome, win
vincīre -nxisse -nctum — tie
vinc(u)lum -ī n — bond, chain
vindicāre — claim, avenge
vīnea -ae f — vineyard, mantlet
vīnum -ī n — wine
violāre — violate
violentus -a -um, adv -nter — violent, impetuous
vir -ī m — man, husband
vīrēs -ium f pl — strength
virga -ae f — rod
virginitās -ātis f — virginity
virgō -inis f — maiden, young girl
virīlis -e — male
virītim — man by man, evenly
virtūs -ūtis f — valor, courage
vīs, acc vim, abl vī — force, violence, power, value, quantity, number
viscera -um n pl — internal organs

vīs ?-sisse — go and see, visit
vīs ?-ī n — sight
vīs -ūs m — sight
vīt ae f — life
vīt ? — avoid
vīt is f — vine, centurion's staff
vit n -ī n — defect, fault, vice
vit erāre — criticize, blame
vīv e vīxisse — live, be alive
vīv -a -um — living, alive, live
vix — hardly
vix um — scarcely yet, only just
vo ?ulum -ī n — word
vō is -is f — vowel
vo e — call, summon, invite
v re in +acc — bring into, expose to
vo e — fly
vo re — fly about, flutter
vo ris -is f — bird
vo tārius -a -um — voluntary
vo tās -ātis f — will
vo tās -ātis f — pleasure, delight
vo īre — roll, *pass* whirl
vo re -visse volūtum — roll, turn (over), ponder, *pass* turn, revolve
vo ?ō -inis f — abyss, whirlpool
vo e — swallow, devour
vō ?bīs — you, yourselves
vō ?et — you, yourselves
vo e vōvisse vōtum — promise, vow
vō ōcis f — voice
vu ris -e — common, everyday
vu adv — commonly
vu s -ī n — the (common) people
vu rāre — wound
vu s -eris n — wound
vu r -is m — vulture
vu ?-ūs m — countenance, face

Z
zej ?rus -ī m — west wind
zō -ae f — girdle, zone

GRAMMATICAL TERMS

LATIN	ABBREVIATIONS	ENGLISH
ablātīvus (cāsus)	*abl*	ablative
accūsātīvus (cāsus)	*acc*	accusative
āctīvum (genus)	*āct*	active
adiectīvum (nōmen)	*adi*	adjective
adverbium -ī *n*	*adv*	adverb
appellātīvum (nōmen)		appellative
cāsus -ūs *m*		case
comparātiō -ōnis *f*		comparison
comparātīvus (gradus)	*comp*	comparative
coniugātiō -ōnis *f*		conjugation
coniūnctiō -ōnis *f*	*coni*	conjunction
coniūnctīvus (modus)	*coni*	subjunctive
datīvus (cāsus)	*dat*	dative
dēclīnātiō -ōnis *f*	*dēcl*	declension
dēmōnstrātīvum (prōnōmen)		demonstrative
dēpōnentia (verba)	*dēp*	deponent
fēminīnum (genus)	*f, fēm*	feminine
futūrum (tempus)	*fut*	future
futūrum perfectum (tempus)	*fut perf*	future perfect
genetīvus (cāsus)	*gen*	genitive
genus (nōminis/verbī)		gender/voice
gerundium -ī *n/* gerundīvum -ī *n*		gerund/gerundive
imperātīvus (modus)	*imp, imper*	imperative
imperfectum (tempus praeteritum)	*imperf*	imperfect
indēclinābile (vocābulum)	*indēcl*	indeclinable
indēfinītum (prōnōmen)		indefinite
indicātīvus (modus)	*ind*	indicative
īnfinītīvus (modus)	*īnf*	infinitive
interiectiō -ōnis *f*		interjection
interrogātīvum (prōnōmen)		interrogative
locātīvus (cāsus)	*loc*	locative
masculīnum (genus)	*m, masc*	masculine
modus (verbī)		mode
neutrum (genus)	*n, neutr*	neuter
nōminātīvus (cāsus)	*nōm*	nominative
optātīvus (modus)		optative
pars ōrātiōnis		part of speech
participium -ī *n*	*part*	participle
passīvum (genus)	*pass*	passive
perfectum (tempus praeteritum)	*perf*	perfect
persōna -ae *f*	*pers*	person
persōnāle (prōnōmen)		personal
plūrālis (numerus)	*pl, plūr*	plural
plūsquamperfectum (tempus praet.)	*plūsqu*	pluperfect
positīvus (gradus)	*pos*	positive
possessīvum (prōnōmen)		possessive
praepositiō -ōnis *f*	*prp, praep*	preposition
praesēns (tempus)	*praes*	present
praeteritum (tempus)	*praet*	preterite, past tense
prōnōmen -inis *n*	*prōn*	pronoun
proprium (nōmen)		proper name
relātīvum (prōnōmen)	*rel*	relative
singulāris (numerus)	*sg, sing*	singular
superlātīvus (gradus)	*sup*	superlative
supīnum		supine
tempus (verbī)		tense
verbum	*vb*	verb
vocātīvus (cāsus)	*voc*	vocative